A reflective resource for
performance management

Effective Teachers
in Primary Schools

Second Edition

Tony Swainston

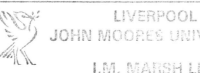

network
continuum

Continuum International Publishing Group
Network Continuum
The Tower Building
11 York Road
London
SE1 7NX

80 Maiden Lane, Suite 704
New York
NY 10038

www.networkcontinuum.co.uk
www.continuumbooks.com

© Tony Swainston 2008

British Library Cataloguing-in-Publication Data
A catalogue record for this book is available from the British Library.
ISBN: 9781855394629 (paperback)

Library of Congress Cataloging-in-Publication Data
A catalog record for this book is available from the Library of Congress

Typeset by Fakenham Photosetting Limited, Fakenham, Norfolk
Printed and bound in Great Britain by CPI Antony Rowe

Effective Teachers in Primary Schools

Second Edition

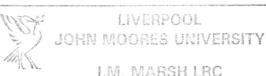

Other titles by Tony Swainston

Effective Teachers in Secondary Schools (2nd edition) – Tony Swainston
Effective Leadership in Schools – Tony Swainston
Behaviour Management – Tony Swainston

Contents

About the author

Tony Swainston taught for 20 years in three comprehensive schools. During this time as well as being a physics teacher he had a number of roles including pastoral head of year and assistant headteacher. He completed the NPQH (National Professional Qualification for Headteachers) before working for the DfES and then the TDA for three years as a Regional CPD Adviser. In 2006 he set up his own consultancy, E.C.M. Connections Ltd. The central focus of E.C.M. Connections is that Every Citizen Matters and the core belief is in the tremendous potential of each individual. E.C.M. Connections Ltd works to develop the efficacy of individuals, the collective effectiveness of groups and the culture of whole organizations and communities. (Visit www.ecmconnections.co.uk)

Through E.C.M. Connections Ltd Tony is a Regional CPD Adviser for Teachers TV. He is also a Project Director for The Pacific Institute, which focuses on the management of change, effective leadership, setting goals to achieve results and thinking in ways that create success.

Tony's work in education now includes running leadership training programmes for headteachers and other leaders, effective teacher and behaviour courses for teachers and coaching throughout a wide spectrum of school staff. He also trains facilitators who then work with parents through a programme called STEPS.

Tony is a highly sought after facilitator and speaker. He has spoken internationally to educational leaders in six countries about 'The Teacher as the Lead Learner'.

Tony's wife teaches French and they have three children.

You can contact Tony at tony.swainston@ecmconnections.co.uk

Acknowledgements

I am eternally grateful to the six teachers in Effective Teachers in Primary Schools who agreed for me to film them in their classrooms. From initial discussions with Gervase Phinn 11 years ago, when he was a Senior Adviser in North Yorkshire, the seed of an idea that developed into the VITAL (Visually Instructive Teaching And Learning) project was planted. I am thankful to Gervase for the encouragement he gave me at that time. Instrumental in the development of the VITAL project have also been John Freeman (a Senior Adviser in Leeds), Chris Edwards (the Chief Executive of Education Leeds), Anne Clarke (headteacher of Benton Park School in Leeds) and Elspeth Jones (Dean at Leeds Met University). All of these have given me tremendous encouragement and support.

Four people who became good friends carried out the filming and editing of all of the material for the VITAL project. They are Mike Hooper, Andy Riley, Bob Bajorek and Paul Wilmott from Leeds Met University. Thanks also to John Lynch from Leeds Met for organizing all of the filming.

Preface to the new edition

A changing view that looks the same

Over the past year I have run a number of CPD programmes for a broad spectrum of teachers. These have been based around my personal research and writing, much of which is an integral part of *Effective Teachers in Primary Schools* and *Effective Teachers in Secondary Schools*. The wonderful groups I have had the privilege to work with have had a range of experience from being headteachers to ITT students and NQTs. Working with teachers and seeking to answer the question 'what is an effective teacher?' has been exciting, rewarding and revealing. The exciting and rewarding aspects of the work I do with teachers are due to the journey of discovery I go on with each of the groups I work with. All teachers are intrigued by the possibility of beginning to unfold the multifarious nature of teaching and learning. Teaching is something that teachers do each day yet they rarely have the opportunity to reflect on some of the fundamental building blocks of effective teaching. That is not to say that any one teacher will not have strong opinions about what constitutes effective teaching. It is just that when they begin to discuss and challenge these ideas with other teachers they begin to realize that at times their views may have been based on limited observation, intuition and common sense. In this way we can all develop beliefs about teaching that can become our personal reality. At times we all need to challenge these ideas. We may find that afterwards we still hold the same view but through discussion, analysis, experimentation and reflection we are now able more clearly to articulate why we hold these views. The revealing aspect of the work I do with teachers comes from the views that they express about the nature of effective teaching. Exploring and sharing ideas about effective teaching always generates enthusiasm. Many of the aspects that are covered generate views where agreement is swiftly reached. Other ideas about what constitutes effective teaching initiate discussions that can often polarize different individuals or groups. One of the interesting things about this is that some of the skills or characteristics that the members of one group agree on as being fundamental to being an effective teacher will be the very things in another group that cause the greatest diversity of views. You may therefore ask the question 'can we ever come to an absolute agreement about what effective teaching sounds, looks and feels like?'

My response to this is that we will never reach a situation where everyone agrees on the constituent elements of an effective teacher. Anyone who has been a teacher and taken part in a whole school or departmental meeting will know how difficult it can be to arrive at a unanimous view on just about any issue. However, I do think that we can move towards a situation where the majority will agree on a set of fundamental skills and characteristics that are observable in effective teachers.

The purpose of *Effective Teachers in Primary Schools* is to provide material that helps us towards a deeper understanding of what constitutes effective teaching. In doing this we will begin to share a common language that helps us to talk to each other in a more informed way about the building blocks of effective teaching. Since the first edition of *Effective Teachers in Primary Schools* was published five years ago schools have gone through many changes. Our views about the most suitable curriculum for the young people we are educating for the world of tomorrow may be changing as well. Throughout all the change there is one thing that remains constant. That is that teachers do make a difference to the lives of young people. The teaching skills, professional characteristics and personality of each teacher will impact on pupils in an often profound way. Knowing this it seems clear to me that we must constantly strive to understand more about how we can all become better teachers. I have met many brilliant teachers over the past 25 years. The one characteristic they all share is the desire they have to become even better at what they do. They are their own greatest critics. They maintain their high levels of teaching competence by constantly considering what they do, experimenting and taking risks with new ideas and clearly demonstrating to classes that they are in a partnership of learning.

The journey is exciting but never ending. Just as the complexity of life itself will always raise more questions than answers for us so it is with teaching. This is not surprising because a key part of teaching is to do with communication and human interaction. A quote from Malcolm Boyd describes what is in effect a key purpose of teaching:

> *Real answers need to be found in dialogue and interaction and, yes, our shared human condition. This means being open to one another instead of simply fighting to maintain a prescribed position.*

This also describes the philosophy that underpins the purpose of *Effective Teachers*. So things may change in some ways in education but effective teaching, through effective communication and interaction that leads to learning and the answers to fundamental questions, will always be needed in our schools.

Using the *Professional Standards for Teachers*

In 2007 the TDA published *Professional Standards for Teachers. Why sit still in your career?* These standards attempt to give a sense of continuity and progression through the potential stages of a teacher's professional life.

The TDA website says:

> *The standards will help teachers to review their professional practice, inform their career decisions and identify their professional development needs. Where teachers wish to progress to the next career stage, the next level of the framework provides a reference point for all teachers when considering future development.*

The professional standards cover the following career stages:

- ▸ **Q** = qualified teacher status
- ▸ **C** = core standards for main scale teachers who have successfully completed their induction
- ▸ **P** = post-threshold teachers on the upper pay scale
- ▸ **E** = excellent teachers
- ▸ **A** = advanced skills teachers (ASTs).

The standards are arranged in three interrelated sections:

- ▸ professional **attributes**

- professional **knowledge and understanding**, and
- professional **skills**.

The standards show clearly what is expected at each career stage.

Again the TDA website informs us that

> *Each set of standards builds on the previous set, so that a teacher being considered for the threshold would need to satisfy the threshold standards* **(P)** *and meet the core standards* **(C)***; a teacher aspiring to become an excellent teacher would need to satisfy the standards that are specific to that status* **(E)** *and meet the preceding standards* **(C and P)***; and a teacher aspiring to become an AST would need to satisfy the standards that are specific to that status* **(A)** *as well as meeting the preceding standards* **(C, P and E)** *– although they can apply for an AST post before going through the threshold.*

The standards should be used as a backdrop to performance management discussions

Teachers' performance should be viewed in relation to their current career stage and the career stage they are approaching. The relevant standards should be looked at as a whole in order to help teachers identify areas of strength and areas for further professional development.

Professional standards provide the backdrop to discussions about performance and future development. The standards define the professional attributes, knowledge, understanding and skills for teachers at each career stage.

How have the standards been developed?

The TDA has a role in bringing coherence to the framework of professional and occupational standards for classroom teachers. This has involved a review of standards for qualified teacher status (QTS), induction, threshold and advanced skills teacher, and the development of standards for the excellent teacher scheme.

From September 2005, the TDA conducted consultations online and through national conferences. Over 7,000 people from the profession responded.

How the standards and the Hay McBer analysis of teacher effectiveness compare

When the DfES (now DCSF) financed Hay McBer Report was published in 2000 it set out clearly the aspects of what makes a teacher effective in the classroom. To assist analysis it divides the observed effectiveness of a teacher into three aspects: teaching skills, professional characteristics and classroom climate. The three aspects of the Professional Standards for Teachers are: professional attributes, professional knowledge and understanding and professional skills. The table below shows the comparison.

Hay McBer	Professional Standards
Teaching skills	Professional attributes
Professional Characteristics	Professional knowledge and understanding
Classroom Climate	Professional skills

So what is the link between the two? The simple answer to this is that the *Professional Standards for Teachers* deals with the broad and holistic nature of the role of the teacher as a professional in a school whereas the Hay McBer Report looks more closely at what the teacher is doing in the classroom that results in them being effective classroom practitioners. The standards cover both the role the teacher has in the classroom and in addition the role they play in the broader context of a school. These include the themes of developing professional and constructive relationships, working within the law and frameworks and professional knowledge and understanding. These are all aspects that impact on the effectiveness of the teacher in the classroom but they are not things that can be easily identified and observed in the classroom. The three themes run throughout the professional standards.

In terms of the theme of developing professional and constructive relationships the TDA says the rationale is as follows:

> *The education and well-being of children and young people increasingly involves groups of teachers, support staff and other professionals working in schools and across a range of children's services to support learners to fulfil their educational potential, develop positive values and attitudes and become confident, contributing members of society. The learning and development needs of all children and young people are better met when teachers develop constructive, respectful relationships with colleagues, learners and their parents or carers, founded on effective and considered communication, collaboration and high expectations of all.*

In terms of the theme of working within the law the TDA says the rationale is as follows:

> *Teachers have legal obligations, rights and contractual entitlements as employees to work within the law and frameworks in order to protect and safeguard the rights and well-being of learners and colleagues. Legislation, statutory and non-statutory frameworks exist to ensure not only that all children and young people receive their educational entitlement but also to protect and safeguard their well-being, both in schools and beyond.*

In terms of the theme of frameworks and professional knowledge and understanding the TDA says the rationale is as follows:

> *All children and young people, irrespective of background and ability, have a right to receive support, guidance and challenge tailored to their specific needs and abilities. Teachers will be more able to respond to the individual needs of learners, enabling them to make better progress, if they have an understanding and knowledge of how attainment can be raised and the many factors that influence children and young people's well-being, development and ability to learn.*

There are, however, clear links between the Hay McBer Report and the standards where the standards are referring directly to the practice of the teacher in the classroom. The Hay McBer Report and the observation forms that are provided within this book can therefore be used to carry out classroom observations. The results of these can then be linked to the standards and used to give very detailed professional feedback to teachers with a common language used that is specific rather than general. This then leads on to meaningful performance management objectives that can be discussed and which relate to classroom effectiveness. The diagram below illustrates this process.

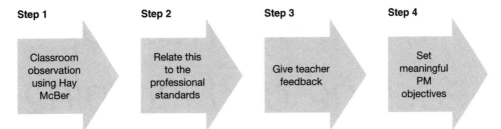

Step 1 Classroom observation using Hay McBer

Step 2 Relate this to the professional standards

Step 3 Give teacher feedback

Step 4 Set meaningful PM objectives

Using the Hay McBer analysis sheets that have been specially designed for *Effective Teachers* and for classroom observations it is therefore possible to acquire detailed material that can then be linked to the professional standards. The DVD resources and analysis within this book provide guidance on how it is possible to match what we may observe in the classroom with the elements of the Hay McBer Report. All the forms at the back of this book can be downloaded in PDF form from Tony Swainston's website: www.ecmconnections.co.uk

'It is one of the great ironies: schools are in the business of teaching and learning, yet they are terrible at learning from each other. If they ever discover how to do this, their future is assured.'

Michael Fullan (2001)

Section 1

Introduction

This section concerns the following.

▸▸ **Teachers count**

A look at how the role of the teacher is changing while fundamentals remain the same.

▸▸ **An overview of the Hay McBer Report**

A Model of Teacher Effectiveness: Report by Hay McBer to the Department for Education and Employment, June 2000 is used here as a framework for the analysis of the teachers filmed.

▸▸ **How *Effective Teachers in Primary Schools* can be used by schools and teachers**

The different ways in which this book and the accompanying videos can be used in primary schools are outlined. In addition, this resource will be of value to secondary schools.

▸▸ **The key messages in *Effective Teachers in Primary Schools***

The basis of what the VITAL project, on which this resource is based, can tell us.

▸▸ **The value in being a reflective practitioner**

The value of continuously looking at our practice as teachers.

▸▸ **Do teachers really make a difference?**

What research tells us – and what we may already know instinctively.

▸▸ **Secondary and primary school teachers – the similarities and differences**

What research says about this and what the evidence from the VITAL project tells us.

Teachers count

I hope that as you watch the teachers in the videos accompanying this book you, like me, will be impressed by their professionalism and dedication. In an age of rapid change, my admiration for teachers never diminishes. And despite all the changes that are happening in education at the moment, there are aspects of being an effective teacher that remain constant. I believe that there is something magical, something wonderful, about a teacher who is operating effectively with a class of young people. It is about sharing an experience, sharing a joy of learning and sharing a journey of discovery. It is about the complex mix of human personal interaction and nurtured relationships that – when it works well – makes a lesson flow with purpose and direction.

Teachers will, in the future, adapt their teaching to accommodate the exciting and apparently never-ending advances of ICT in the classroom. But as the DfES document *Time for Standards: Reforming the school workforce* (2002) makes clear:

> *ICT cannot do a teacher's job. The computer is not a replacement for a teacher.*

ICT will of course impact significantly on education and the DfES document goes on to add that ICT:

> *... is a tool which can make teachers and teaching more powerful. And it can free up valuable teacher time. Cutting-edge ICT plus teacher creativity adds up to a heady mixture in stretching pupils' imaginations.*

But the role of the teacher is far too special to be replaced by a machine.

You will see in *Effective Teachers in Primary Schools* two valuable examples of how teachers use ICT in their classrooms to enhance the learning experience of their pupils. But these teachers also display many essential characteristics as effective classroom practitioners that combine with the use of computers to create the whole teaching and learning experience. You will also be able to see a teacher using certain 'accelerated learning' techniques including music and visualization. These techniques are truly wonderful to witness, but again this teacher displays a wealth of other Teaching Skills and Professional Characteristics (as they are termed in the Hay McBer Report – see Section Five), which ensure that the lesson as a whole – the teaching and learning experience – is successful.

Effective Teachers in Primary Schools is about looking at teachers and reflecting on what makes teachers effective. Every teacher is unique, every teacher is special and every teacher is a leader in his or her classroom. Every teacher is able to shape the future of the precious individuals he or she teaches while influencing the future direction of education as a whole. Before resigning as Secretary of State for Education in October 2002, Estelle Morris said:

> *We have the best generation ever of teachers.*

The VITAL project and the books and videos that have been produced as a result are, in some small way, a celebration of all these teachers. It was a privilege for me to be able to watch each and every one of the primary school teachers you will see in the videos accompanying this book. I learned a great deal by watching these true professionals. I hope that you too will enjoy and learn from watching them in action and reflecting on your own teaching practice.

Ben: '*I like my teacher to be nice.*'

An overview of the Hay McBer Report

A Model of Teacher Effectiveness: Report by Hay McBer to the Department for Education and Employment, June 2000 is a major piece of educational research commissioned by the UK government. The VITAL project (of which *Effective Teachers in Primary Schools* represents the second stage) seeks to use the findings of the Hay McBer Report, along with other educational research, to make it clear through video evidence what makes a teacher effective in the classroom.

There is also a clear link made between the Professional Standards for Teachers and the Hay McBer Report. The VITAL series can therefore be used as a major tool to assist Performance Management and school improvement.

The website tells us:

> *Effective teachers in the future will need to deal with a climate of continual change and foster a framework of continual improvement, embracing openness and integration. The Model of Teacher Effectiveness: Report by Hay McBer to the DfEE, June 2000 was designed to provide a framework describing effective teaching and be part of the modernising of the teaching profession. The research used complementary data-collection techniques involving a representative sample of schools and broad range of teachers, and aimed for coherence with other recent educational research.*

The value of the Hay McBer Report in terms of the VITAL work is that it provides a clear framework for the analysis of each of the teachers filmed. As the statement above indicates, there is coherence between the findings of the Hay McBer Report and other educational research.

How *Effective Teachers in Primary Schools* can be used by schools and teachers

Effective Teachers (Network Educational Press, 2002) is based upon the first stage of the VITAL project, which concentrated on secondary school teachers. This resource, *Effective Teachers in Primary Schools*, is the product of VITAL Stage 2, and concentrates on primary school teachers. It will therefore be of use to primary schools in a number of ways – for example, schools could use it as:

- ▸ a useful resource for ITT/GTP/SCITT students in the school. ITT/GTP/SCITT students can use the video evidence of a range of effective teachers along with the analysis in this book to help them reflect on their own views on teaching.

- ▸ a resource to be used by any teachers in the school who, in a similar way, would like to reflect on their own teaching – what they do well and what they might decide to develop. Teachers may wish to take *Effective Teachers in Primary Schools* home and look at it in their own time.

- ▸ a resource to be used during staff training days. Again, the book and videos can provide a stimulus for reflection about the art and science of teaching. They should also, hopefully, provoke vigorous discussion, which itself can be very useful.

- ▸ a link between effective classroom teaching, the Professional Standards for Teachers, performance management and school improvement.

- ▸ coaching of colleagues in the art of effective teaching.

In addition, secondary schools may well find that they can learn a lot by looking at the primary school teachers on the videos. There is at the moment some concern to ensure that the transition from KS2 to KS3 is as smooth as possible. This is more likely to be the case if secondary school teachers have an understanding of the type and level of work that goes on in primary school classes.

Have you ever wondered what an effective teacher looks like? In schools we talk about teachers being 'effective' but what does this mean? The VITAL project aims to reveal what effective teaching is all about. Some of the teachers on the videos will almost certainly appeal to you more than others – probably because they tend to match your own preferred range of Teaching Skills and Professional Characteristics. All the teachers are very different but what they all do, in their own unique ways, is operate as effective teachers.

The key messages in *Effective Teachers in Primary Schools*

The key messages to come through from the VITAL project are outlined below.

1 Although most teachers are often doing a really good job, they may not always value the personal skills, knowledge and talents they possess as much as they should. Teachers can often be their own biggest critics. The VITAL video evidence of effective teachers in action, together with the analysis in this book, will hopefully make teachers more consciously aware of their own teaching.

2 The various elements that combine to make an effective teacher are revealed in *Effective Teachers in Primary Schools*. Research on teacher effectiveness is used as the basis of the analysis. Most important, however, is that real teachers in real classrooms make this research directly relevant to practising teachers.

3 We can all improve. No matter how good we are, there is always room to develop the skills, knowledge and talents we possess. A good way of doing this is by observing other teachers in action. *Effective Teachers in Primary Schools* provides a vehicle for this and encourages teachers to become reflective practitioners.

The value in being a reflective practitioner

Improving as teachers allows us to do the job better and reduces levels of stress. This empowers us as teachers and enables us to empower the pupils we teach to become more active and less passive in their individual learning.

Can you conceive of a situation where top class athletes, professional footballers or tennis players never trained to hone their skills and that the only time they ran, jumped or played their game was during competition? Of course not – in reality, professional sports men and women train constantly. David Beckham refines his obvious natural talent through dedicated training so that the hours of practice bring about periodic moments of apparent genius. And it is now well acknowledged that the psychological aspect of any sport plays a great part in determining performance. In a similar way, we would be horrified if, after their initial period of training, doctors and surgeons never updated their skills and knowledge.

Teaching, too, should be viewed as a lifelong learning profession where new and old or established ideas on teaching are constantly assessed and experimented with. The ideal situation would be for teachers to be involved in their own personal classroom research. This could either be on a very small and personal level with the teacher using action research with a single class to investigate a certain idea, or alternatively part of a larger project. The benefits to the individual teacher of either using or being involved in research are immense. Teachers carrying out research are able to reflect on their own teaching, and on teaching in general. The process of reflection is vital. It is hoped that the VITAL material in *Effective Teachers in Primary Schools* will assist teachers in this process.

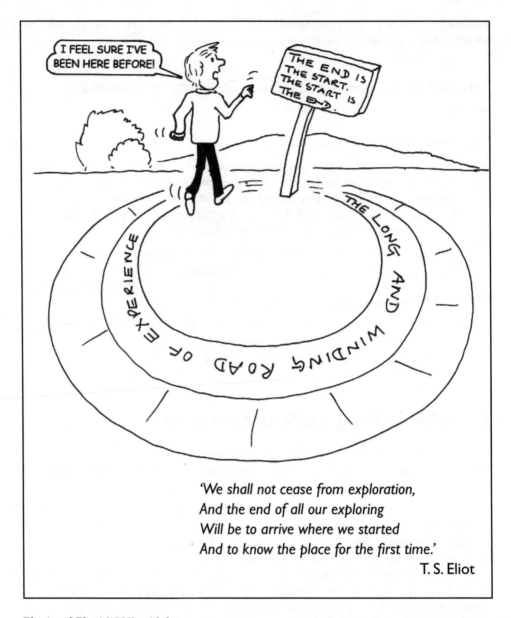

'We shall not cease from exploration,
And the end of all our exploring
Will be to arrive where we started
And to know the place for the first time.'

T. S. Eliot

Blasé and Blasé (1998) said that:

> *Reflective practice is founded on the assumption that increased awareness of one's professional performance can result in considerable improvements of performance. Specifically, reflection on teaching has been advocated by many as a means to question teaching/learning events in order to bring one's teaching actions to a conscious level, to interpret the consequences of one's actions, and to conceptualize alternative teaching processes.*

Effective Teachers in Primary Schools looks at what being an effective teacher actually means. Recent research is combined with evidence and analysis of real teachers in their classrooms to try to give a better understanding about this very complex issue.

> *Not to know is bad; not to wish to know is worse.*
>
> *African proverb*

This proverb is one we should remind ourselves of all the time, as teachers. We owe it to ourselves and the pupils we teach continually to seek ways in which we can improve as teachers. We need to demonstrate to the pupils we teach that we want to improve and learn in order to make it clear to them that we really do believe in the concept of becoming lifelong learners.

UNESCO's International Commission on Education for the Twenty-first Century has argued the importance of everyone adopting a lifelong learning approach:

> *Each individual must be equipped to seize learning opportunities throughout life, both to broaden her or his knowledge, skills and attitudes, and to adapt to a changing, complex and interdependent world.*

As lifelong learners, we need to strive to understand the complex process involved in being an effective teacher. *Effective Teachers in Primary Schools* intends to assist teachers in this by providing a resource for reflection so that we can move towards a level of *conscious competence* (see Section Four). Teachers who adopt a reflective practitioner approach, constantly appraising their own classroom techniques – their Teaching Skills and Professional Characteristics, as the Hay McBer Report terms them – will be enriched by the experience and bring vitality into their own lessons. A great way of helping teachers to reflect is to engage in observing other teachers in action. This happens in certain schools already but even in these schools it is sometimes difficult to find the time to reflect fully on what is observed. This is where the VITAL material in this resource can be useful. The video material, together with the manual, allows teachers to reflect collectively or individually on classroom practice. The process of analysis adopted in this book provides one possible framework for a considered appraisal of what an effective teacher looks like.

Do teachers really make a difference?

Teaching is a noble profession. Teachers can truly influence the futures of individuals and, as a result, the future of the nation. The task we have is therefore both daunting and exciting. David Miliband (the then UK Minister for School Standards) said, in 2002:

> *I am delighted to have been appointed as an education minister because it allows me to contribute to what I believe is the biggest task facing this country – developing the talents of all our children. If we get our state education system right we can renew our economy and strengthen communities. Get it wrong, accept second-best, and we will be fighting to get anything right in crime, health or the economy.*

These are powerful words and indicate why we must constantly look at our own practice and seek to find the most efficient and effective ways of developing the precious art and science of teaching. Many people say that young people today are very different from those of 10 or 15 years ago. To some extent this may be true. The world has changed and children and their behaviour reflect the way in which they have had to adapt to these changes. In many respects, however, the fundamental needs and desires of young people are the same as they have always been. They will respond now, as they always have done, to teachers whose lessons feature:

- work focus (most pupils on task most of the time)
- strong academic emphasis
- clarity of goals for pupil learning
- pupil responsibility (independent learning is encouraged)
- challenge for pupils of *all* ability levels
- teacher enthusiasm
- effective classroom control
- promptness in starting and finishing
- regular monitoring of pupil progress.

In addition, children want to feel that the teacher understands them – or at least makes some attempt to do so.

The question of whether teachers make a difference was investigated in 1995 by OFSTED, QCA and the TTA through organized regional conferences. Research linked with this indicated a number of factors relating to teacher effectiveness similar to those stated above.

- Although there is no one right way to teach, teachers can enhance their general effectiveness when their teaching is purposeful, efficient, clear, structured and adaptive.
- High expectations by teachers are of utmost importance.
- Good teaching involves more than just exposition and arranging activities.
- Good teaching is more than the mere transmission of subject knowledge.
- An effective learning environment is orderly, stimulating, attractive, safe and supportive.
- Planning and pupil participation are important factors in effective lessons.
- Learning to learn entails increasing the scope for pupils to use their initiative and to develop a capacity for independent work across the age range.
- Effective teaching and learning regularly features a suitable balance between class, group and individual work.
- Effective learning occurs when pupils are given opportunities to apply the knowledge and skills they are taught.
- Effective learning design allows pupils to summarize what they have experienced and to reflect carefully on this experience.
- Effective teaching is complemented by fair discipline, positive reinforcement and explicit, formative feedback.

Teachers can have a significant impact on the development of individuals. Teachers really do make a difference – educational research confirms this – and this is why we must all try to become more effective classroom practitioners.

Secondary and primary school teachers – the similarities and differences

Effective Teachers in Primary Schools was produced following the success of *Effective Teachers in Secondary Schools*. A number of primary school teachers said they valued the process of using *Effective Teachers* and would welcome a similar resource showing effective primary teachers in action. However, as has already been suggested, secondary school teachers will also benefit from using this second VITAL resource – as teachers, we can all benefit from looking at each other's practice. In particular, secondary school teachers may enjoy looking at how primary school teachers have adapted their teaching to accommodate the literacy and numeracy initiatives.

But what are the differences between the techniques employed by teachers in secondary and primary schools? Are there different Teaching Skills, Professional Characteristics and Classroom Climates that are evident? In my opinion, there do not appear to be any major differences.

Clearly, primary school teachers tend, on the whole (but not exclusively), to teach one class throughout the course of the year. This enables primary school teachers to get to know the pupils they teach far better. They will, as a result, be more able to respond to the specific needs of each individual on a daily basis. A primary school teacher will also be able to set out his or her own consistent expectations for the class, whereas in a secondary school the class will encounter four, five or six teachers each day, all with different approaches and expectations.

However, it still seems to be the case that good teachers – effective teachers – achieve success in very similar ways, no matter what the phase of the group they are teaching, or the subject. The skills and characteristics possessed by effective teachers appear to be consistent across all phases and subjects. From his syntheses of reviews of studies in different curriculum areas (mainly reading, maths and science), Fraser (1989) concludes that effects are similar in primary, junior high and high school studies. Given this, he suggests that there is more justification for assuming that there is generality across subjects, than for assuming that there are specific teaching practices associated with different subjects.

Fraser's conclusion reinforces the fact that we can indeed all learn from each other. This includes looking at teachers across different phases of education and teaching a variety of subjects. The rich resource we have – the expertize of the teachers in all our schools – must be used to help us all to understand more about the complexity of teaching and, as a result, make us all into better teachers.

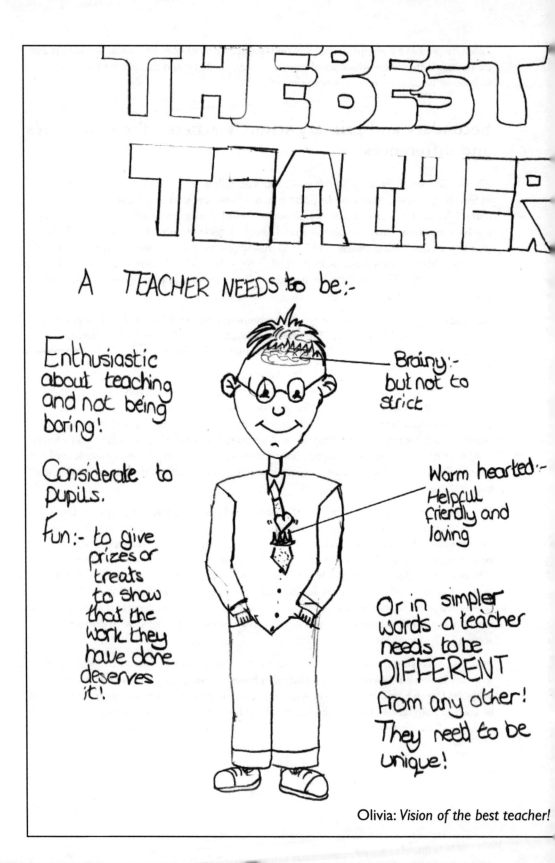

Olivia: *Vision of the best teacher!*

Section 2

What an effective teacher looks like

This section concerns the following.

▶▶ **The difficulty of defining 'effectiveness'**

Differential success in different circumstances can make defining effectiveness problematic.

▶▶ **Are certain teaching styles more effective?**

The debate over different teaching styles has sometimes confused the issue of teacher effectiveness.

▶▶ **Factors that influence effectiveness**

Research indicates that there are certain things that influence teacher effectiveness.

▶▶ **The burden of the assessment culture**

How an over-emphasis on assessment could be negatively influencing teaching and learning.

▶▶ **What is meant by effective teaching?**

An indication that effective teaching is not linked with examination success.

▶▶ **Different ways of being effective**

There is not just one way of being an effective teacher. Every teacher is unique.

'Teaching should
be such that
what is offered is
perceived as
a valuable gift
and not as
a hard duty.'

Albert Einstein

The difficulty of defining 'effectiveness'

OFSTED inspectors, advisers and the like have a great privilege in being able to enter many classrooms and, as a result, may arrive – in their own minds at least – at some understanding of what an effective teacher looks like. Many teachers, on the other hand, may not believe that they fully understand the elements that combine to make an effective teacher. An aim of the VITAL materials in *Effective Teachers in Primary Schools* is to remove this mystery. You can look at the teachers in the videos accompanying this book and then study in a variety of ways the different aspects of effective teaching that they display.

When research has been done on what an effective teacher looks like, the picture can become very complex. There are, for example, equity implications. Most teachers experience the frustration of apparent success with one class and comparative failure with another. What does this tell us? Is the teacher effective or not? In addition to *differential effectiveness* with different pupil groups, some teachers claim to have greater success in general with boys than girls, or vice versa. But again gender is not the end of the story. Socio-economic status (SES) and ethnicity of particular pupil groups are other areas that may influence the effectiveness of teachers. This therefore raises the question of what we mean when we are talking about 'effective teachers'.

To try to avoid this potential difficulty, we can look at generic aspects of teaching that tend to combine to produce effective teaching. This is what the VITAL materials aim to do.

Are certain teaching styles more effective?

Some people have tried to define teacher effectiveness by concentrating on their teaching styles. These are sometimes contrasted as follows:

- formal lessons and informal lessons
- traditional and so-called 'progressive' lessons
- individual and whole-class teaching.

There has been a great debate about the relative merits of each of these approaches. So which styles are the best? This is really an impossible question to answer except to say that all of these styles can be employed successfully and that perhaps a teacher who employs a mixture of the different teaching styles at different times is the ideal. Effective teachers know when they need to employ a certain teaching style with a certain class or, indeed, how they need to vary their approach with the same class. (Dale Robinson, one of the teachers filmed for *Effective Teachers in Primary Schools*, mentions this in his interview session.)

Sammons and co-workers (1995) carried out a review of the *Key Characteristics of Effective Schools* and concluded that an attempt to define teacher effectiveness in terms of the categories above was over-crude and simplistic given the highly complex nature of teacher behaviours.

This should not be viewed by anyone as an argument to be used against looking at new methods or approaches to teaching. Clearly, it is also not the basis of an argument that suggests that teachers should not reflect on their practice. In my view, reflection is absolutely crucial. Teaching has got to be viewed as a lifelong learning process for all teachers. You will be interested to know that, of the eleven important factors identified in the *Key Characteristics of Effective Schools* review, Sammons and co-workers argued that the quality of teaching and expectations had the most significant role to play in fostering pupils' learning and progress and, therefore, their educational outcomes. And so research confirms what we all know: teachers really do make a difference.

Factors that influence effectiveness

Research undertaken by Scheerens (1992) identified 'structured teaching' as being particularly relevant to promoting cognitive attainment in the basic skills. This is apparently especially true in schools serving higher proportions of socio-economically disadvantaged pupils. Characteristics of structured teaching include the following:

▸ making clear what has to be learned

▸ splitting teaching material into manageable units for pupils and offering these in a well-considered sequence

▸ much exercise material in which pupils make use of 'hunches' and prompts

▸ regularly testing for progress with immediate feedback of the results.

On the other hand, it is *not* a good idea to base teacher effectiveness primarily on examination results. An obvious reason for this is that it is impossible to make a comparison between teachers teaching different classes in different year groups (some of which may not even take examinations). We all know that teaching has got to be about more than this. Effective teachers nurture a belief in a pupil that education is worthwhile. They help pupils to understand that learning is a lifelong process. They inspire, motivate and stimulate pupils. They improve the capacity of pupils to learn.

Sackney (in Townsend, Clarke and co-workers, 1999) says:

> *At the heart of the learning process is the quality of the relationships that exist, for in the end it may not be what marks the students attain, but how they feel about themselves and others.*

This brings us on to the difficulty of teaching and learning in a world where so much emphasis is placed on achieving targets.

The burden of the assessment culture

The publication of league tables, and their impact in terms of the future development of a school, has meant that teachers, managers and leaders in schools have all been pushed into concentrating on examination results. In 1999, Watkins pointed out the danger of this when he said that:

> *... a focus on learning can enhance performance, whereas a focus on performance can depress performance.*

However, it appears that we are at the moment stuck in the middle of an *assessment society*. As a result of this, we find that pupils are deeply concerned by the results they attain, teachers are restricted in their teaching by the pressures of achieving externally predicted grades for their students and schools may have their existence threatened by faltering results when compared to performance indicators. If we are not careful, then, schools can be driven to hold success in league tables as their main purpose. A danger associated with this is that the pupils who don't succeed in examination terms can end up with a feeling of failure and rejection. This may have a long-term impact on them and a resultant detrimental impact on society.

Referring to the pupils who don't succeed in conventional examination terms, Mervyn Flecknoe (2002) has said:

> *It is the performance of these low-achieving groups which will determine the economic and social health of society ...*

There is also a danger that we, as teachers, may not always understand the approaches to education of many of the pupils we teach and these pupils are often the ones that fail in our present system of assessment. Goleman (1996) said:

> *Teachers, generally, are those who succeeded in the paper and pencil testing regimes of previous schools; they do not automatically understand the attitudes to education of those whose learning styles are different.*

And again Flecknoe points out the danger of an over-concentration on 'effectiveness' in terms of examination performance:

> *The pursuit of effectiveness could produce an alienated generation of young people who respond unfavourably to measures designed to enable the 'easy to educate' to attain higher test marks.*

One of the main reasons why there has been a concentration on examination results is that these are measurable and therefore it is argued that they can be used to compare schools and individual teachers. The problem is that what many teachers, parents and the general public feel is important in terms of school effectiveness is not measurable. This may include things like happiness, personal autonomy, moral goodness, imagination and civic-mindedness. White (1997) asserts that the 'community at large' is at loggerheads with the school effectiveness researchers because of a disagreement about what it is that we are trying to improve in schooling. Teacher effectiveness that is based on the success of pupils in tests is definitely not what the VITAL project is concerned with.

What is meant by effective teaching?

It is important, therefore, to be clear that when I talk about effective teachers in this resource I am not referring to the narrow measure of effectiveness based on examination outcomes, but rather the broader way in which a teacher inspires, motivates and informs young people so that they can live a rich and varied life and become happy individuals.

This may seem a tall order – and it is. But it illustrates again the importance of the work of teachers.

My view of effective teaching, therefore, embraces the broad way in which teachers can positively influence the approach of pupils to education and, as a result, encourage them to become lifelong learners.

Teachers need to have a sense of self-efficacy in order to teach effectively. They must feel their professional work is bringing about positive change in their pupils. They need to know that, for instance, they are making a difference in the lives of children they are teaching, and that the children are learning. Rudow (1999) said that teachers also need:

> *... to feel wanted, important and in some ways unique, they need to have these needs affirmed by those with whom they live and work.*

Most teachers will feel this deeply and it illustrates clearly the way in which teaching is a highly sensitive and emotionally charged business. Teaching is different from so many other jobs, in a variety of ways, not least of all because it involves the development of so many personal relationships. Many writers have argued that teachers derive their job satisfaction from the psychic rewards of teaching (Lortie, 1975; Rosenholtz, 1989; Hargreaves, 1998). Central among these is the development of close relationships and 'emotional understanding'.

Effective teaching, therefore – in the sense in which I am using the term here – occurs where teachers are nurturing the talents of the pupils they teach to get the very best from them. My view of effective teaching is that, by definition, it requires that effective learning must be taking place. This may result in the pupils achieving good examination results but this is not the only measure by which to judge the teacher. Effective teachers encourage pupils to leave school with the desire to learn more. The pupils are equipped to learn more. When you read in the *Times Educational Supplement* people's comments about the teachers who influenced them most strongly at school, they often refer to the way in which the teacher inspired them with a love of the subject. Often, this inspiration not only encouraged the person to take an interest in that subject, but also stimulated a desire to learn more in general. This is what effective teachers do.

David Miliband (2002) said:

> *Giving every child the chance to make the most of their potential, irrespective of their background, is our number one priority.*
> *We want the best schooling, the great adventure, for all children, not just for those bound to succeed.*

We could easily replace the word 'potential' in David Miliband's statement above with 'strengths'. In my view, the most important tasks a school has are firstly to establish the strengths of each individual pupil, and then to seek to provide an education that will

'Teaching should be such that what is
offered is perceived as a valuable gift
and not as a hard duty.'
Albert Einstein

harness and develop these strengths. This is clearly not an easy thing to achieve, but it is the way for schools to provide an education that matches each individual. This is referred to again later, in Section Three.

Different ways of being effective

Every teacher is different, every teacher is unique and all teachers will move towards being effective in their own ways. In order that we can be as effective as possible as teachers, conscious competence and an understanding of our own strengths have to be our goals. There is a balance to be had between:

- trying new strategies, while at the same time developing certain characteristics we possess that are less effective than we would like, and

- uncovering our strengths and actively working to develop these further.

The VITAL materials in *Effective Teachers in Primary Schools* allow teachers to do both of these things by reflecting on their own practice while watching other teachers.

I would argue that all teachers need to look constantly at good practice in others and be prepared to experiment with new as well as established ideas in teaching. We need to strive for a level of conscious competence in the teaching skills and characteristics of effective teachers. The Hay McBer Report is a useful resource in this respect because it allows the complex nature of teaching to be analysed within certain relatively clearly defined categories. In addition, the VITAL videos accompanying this book enable these categories to be looked at through the real practice of teachers in their classrooms.

The aim is that when teachers look at the VITAL videos they will become more aware of their own strengths. This will give each teacher confidence and allow him or her to work to develop these strength areas.

Davis and Sumara (1997) reject the idea that anyone knows the best way for teachers to behave in any particular circumstance:

> *Relying strictly on some of the popular 'How to' manuals that have been prepared for teacher education programs, one might come to the mistaken conclusion that what it means to teach and how one learns to teach are largely settled.*

This idea may be a comforting thought for all of us as teachers. There is a multitude of ways of achieving success, as VITAL Stage 1 explored in *Effective Teachers*. The VITAL material is certainly not meant to be part of a 'How to' manual – teaching is just too complex to simplify it in this way. *Effective Teachers in Primary Schools* again invites teachers to look at what they do well by observing the same characteristics in other effective teachers. It also allows teachers to look at strategies employed by other teachers, which may be less familiar to them. In some ways, if a teacher looks at the VITAL materials and as a result becomes more conscious of his or her own 'strengths' then success will have been achieved. A teacher who concentrates on these recognized 'strengths' will be equally as rewarded as a teacher who copies and employs new strategies seen in the VITAL materials. Moving towards conscious competence is the ultimate goal. This idea of realizing our own strengths will be a recurrent theme in *Effective Teachers in Primary Schools*, and is expanded in Section Three.

Paige: 'The perfect teacher'

'The object of
education is
to prepare the
young to educate
themselves
throughout
their lives.'

Robert Maynard Hutchins,
President of University of Chicago,
1929–1945

Section 3

Understanding what we can and can't learn

This section concerns the following.

▸▸ **Skills, knowledge and talents**

Understanding the difference between these will help us to focus on the things we are able to refine and develop.

▸▸ **The development of our 'teacher brain'**

There has been a great deal written about how we should approach teaching in terms of the development of the 'pupil brain'. It is equally important to understand how our own 'teacher brain' has developed.

▸▸ **How the VITAL materials can help us to develop our 'teacher brain'**

Using *Effective Teachers in Primary Schools* to help develop a reflective practitioner approach can help us to develop our 'teacher brain'.

Skills, knowledge and talents

To what extent can we learn by looking at other teachers? To what extent can we learn to be better teachers?

To answer these questions we need to understand what sorts of things we are talking about 'learning'. In the book *First, Break all the Rules*, by Marcus Buckingham and Curt Coffman, a distinction is drawn between various categories of attributes that combine to make workers, in whatever sphere, effective in what they do. The book draws on two mammoth research studies undertaken by the Gallup Organization over the past 25 years.

Although it is often the little things that can make a big difference in teaching, we need to know which of these little things we can and cannot teach ourselves or learn from watching other teachers. To understand what we can and can't learn, it is useful at this stage to distinguish between *skills*, *knowledge* and *talents*. Teacher effectiveness is dependent on all of these things.

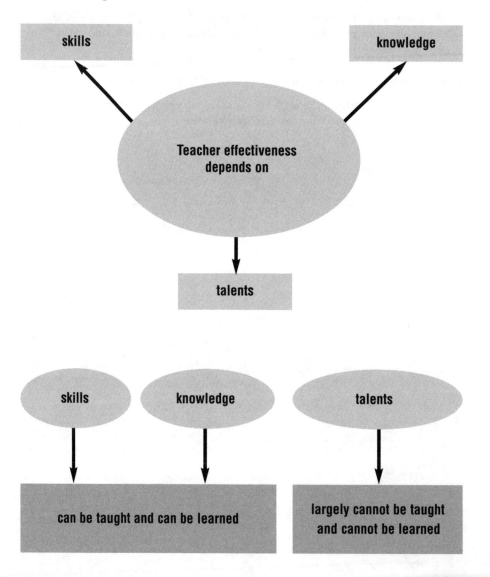

Skills and knowledge comprise things that can be taught and can be learned, whereas talents involve things that largely cannot be taught or learned but that are intrinsic to each person – and perhaps hidden, like buried treasures waiting to be discovered.

The *skills* of a teacher might involve things like:

▸ learning how to use PowerPoint presentations as a way of introducing a lesson

▸ learning how to mark books to a set mark scheme

▸ learning how to give a variety of different kinds of homework, which draw on different modes of research and learning

▸ learning how to structure a lesson to use the time effectively with a variety of activities

▸ learning how to allocate time fairly among pupils.

The *knowledge* of a teacher involves the things that can be acquired over time from reflection, research or experience. These include things like:

▸ acquiring curriculum knowledge and an understanding of curriculum requirements in a subject area

▸ acquiring an understanding of psychological issues to do with pupils and their learning, including methods that can be used to inspire students

▸ acquiring an understanding of sociological issues and how these affect pupils' learning

▸ acquiring an understanding of structural, organizational mechanisms in schools

▸ acquiring an understanding of how weather affects the moods of pupils

▸ acquiring an understanding of how the semiotics of the classroom affect the motivation of pupils

▸ acquiring a growing understanding of the values in schools that are most important.

Talents, on the other hand, are quite different. Talents might include imagination, effective communication, memory, reasoning power, aesthetic sense, physical ability and leadership. Although I agree that certain of these talents may be more difficult to develop in some individuals than in others I would strongly argue that it is possible for everyone to develop in each of these talent areas. The degree of development of any talent will be influenced by a range of factors including the natural inclination of the individuals towards that talent, their development of this talent so far, their awareness of how to develop this talent, their determination to develop in this talent and the opportunities they experience to develop the talent.

I referred earlier to the fact that it is important for schools to try to uncover and then cater for the talents of pupils in schools. It is equally important for teachers to discover their own talents so that they can fully utilize these in the classroom.

What talents are your 'buried treasures'? What talents do these two demonstrate?

The development of our 'teacher brain'

To understand talents, it is important to look at our understanding of how the brain has developed. It is well documented that our knowledge of how the brain works has increased phenomenally over the past few years – we are told that approximately 80 per cent of what we know about how the brain works has been learned in the past 20 years. A great deal of the improved understanding is now being put to good use in lessons and classrooms throughout the UK and around the world.

An understanding of how the brain develops is important for teachers not only in terms of helping children to learn effectively, but also to help them develop their own characteristics as teachers.

The flow chart below is a useful summary of how the brain develops. It illustrates how critical it is for teachers to encourage pupils to develop their 'multiple intelligences' (see Section Four), but also shows how as individuals we may find that certain ways of operating as teachers prove to be hard for us to develop because our brains have not been 'hard-wired' in that way.

1	At birth a child's brain contains one hundred billion neurons – more brain cells than stars in the Milky Way!
2	As a child develops, the neurons grow and die but the number stays roughly the same.
3	The brain cells are the raw material of the mind.
4	But the cells themselves are not the 'mind'. Brain cells are connected together by synapses. It is the pattern of these connections between the cells of the brain that determines the mind.
5	During the first 15 years of life, the synaptic connections start to take shape and dominant features start to develop.
6	From the centre of the brain outwards, neurons send out messages trying to communicate with other neurons and make connections.
7	At three years old, a child may have 15,000 synaptic connections for every one of its one hundred billion neurons.
8	Overload would occur with all this information coming into the brain. A rational approach has to be taken. Some sense has to be made of the information. The way in which sense is made determines the individual.
9	Over the next 10 to 12 years, the network of connections in the brain is refined. Certain synaptic connections grow stronger as they are used more and more. Other synaptic connections become weaker and start to wither away.
10	As a result, an individual is left with his or her own unique set of strong connections. These connections effectively establish the *talents* of the individual.

The brain capacity or potential we all have is truly astounding. This is, of course, the case for all the children we teach as well as for ourselves, and it should provide inspiration for all involved in education.

Dr Harry Chugani, Professor of Neurology at Wayne State University, gives a wonderful analogy to describe what we end up with in our brains as adult individuals. Our strong synaptic connections, he says, are like roads used by a lot of traffic, which get widened as a result. On the other hand, our weak synaptic connections are like roads that are rarely used and consequently fall into disrepair.

Why some synaptic connections become weaker and others stronger is hard to say. It may be due partly to an individual genetic programming propensity we each possess.

Another part may be due to the experiences we encounter as we develop. The balance between *nature* and *nurture* rages on.

Marcus Buckingham and Curt Coffman call the strong synaptic connections our 'four-lane highways'. If you develop a 'four-lane highway' to be someone blessed with empathy for others, then putting yourself in the shoes of someone else and seeing things from their point of view will be no problem. Someone who has a withered empathetic synaptic connection pattern will find that they will struggle in this respect. The 'four-lane highways' are where the enthusiasms of an individual can be found. Along these strong synaptic connections, an individual will speed and produce exciting results. They will excel.

All of this has tremendous repercussions for teaching and learning, of course. Alistair Smith, in his work on 'accelerated learning', describes a variety of techniques that many teachers now find invaluable. As an example, giving a mixture of VAK (Visual, Auditory and Kinesthetic) experiences

Which road would you choose?

in lessons is now the norm for many effective teachers. One way of understanding why this approach is effective is to see that it allows pupils to access information through their preferred 'four-lane highways' of synaptic connections, which then tap into the talents of the pupils.

An understanding of a person's 'four-lane highways' should also influence, in broader terms, the curriculum of that individual. To provide a learning programme that does not match the talents of an individual could be a recipe for disaster. The reasons why certain pupils behave badly in schools are of course very complex, but this kind of mismatch may well have a profound effect. Every individual is different with unique predispositions and a unique set of talents. To cater for each individual is extremely difficult, but at least giving pupils the opportunity to discover their own strengths or talents could pay real dividends in the long term.

Being conscious of our own 'four-lane highways' also has significant bearing on how we should view our development as teachers. Our character is formed by the 'four-lane highways' that have been carved out in our early life, and neuroscience tells us that by our midteens there is a limit to how much these character-determinant neural pathways can be altered. But crucially this does *not* mean that we cannot change as individuals. Skills and knowledge can be learned. Clearly, we need to endeavour to develop the skills and knowledge that will make us more effective teachers. We can grow to understand more about how we operate. We can grow to be more self-aware and to modify and adjust what we do. All is not lost either if we discover that we lack certain talents. We *can* develop these, but must understand that to change them from 'minor country roads' into 'four-lane highways' may be difficult but not impossible. We train ourselves to become competent, but we will really take off and fly by nurturing our unique set of four-lane highway talents.

How the VITAL materials can help us to develop our 'teacher brain'

Looking at the teachers featured in this VITAL resource, we can all reflect on the skills, knowledge and talents they display. Some of these things will comfort us as we recognize them as being part of our own set of skills, knowledge and talents. As I have indicated, some of these things (primarily the skills and knowledge) we can think of learning and developing. Other things – we have called them talents here – we may feel we don't possess in abundance. We can work and develop these. On the other hand our 'four-lane highway' talents can still be developed further and have the potential to greatly empower us. The symphony of our talents significantly determines who we are. This is part of our uniqueness. The realization of this can be invaluable, however. We will arrive at a state of *conscious competence* (referred to throughout this book) about our talents. As a result, we can work on our weaker areas but, more importantly, we can nurture the other rich talents that we do have.

Talents can come in a variety of forms. You may realize that your talents include a capacity for empathy, a seam of patience, an ability to see an opportunity and take a risk, or an ability to influence thought and direction. Whatever your talents are, they should be cared for and nurtured as a precious commodity. Committing yourself to this will enable you to become an even more effective teacher in your unique way. As the Hay McBer Report says:

> *Teachers are not clones. There is, in other words, a multiplicity of ways in which particular characteristics determine how a teacher chooses which approach to use from a repertoire of established techniques in order to influence how pupils feel.*

Once again, this statement should be a great comfort to us. We are all individuals and as such we can all be successful in our own individual way. We can also learn, however, to be better teachers by observing others, either through using resources like those provided in *Effective Teachers in Primary Schools*, or by observing other teachers in our own and other schools. The essential point always to keep in mind is that we can all learn from each other.

Esther: *The cool teacher!*

Section 4

Important factors in becoming effective teachers

This section concerns the following.

‣ **The Kolb cycle**

The Kolb cycle attempts to explain how we learn from experience.

‣ **Unconscious learning**

We should be consciously aware that a lot of our learning happens unconsciously!

‣ **Reflective writing**

How reflective writing can be used as a powerful tool to move towards conscious competence.

‣ **Moving towards a common language and research**

Teachers can begin to share a common language in teaching and learning once the dialogue has started. Classroom-based research is an excellent way of teachers moving towards a common language.

‣ **Emotional intelligence**

The importance of EI for us as teachers and for the pupils we teach.

‣ **Intelligence is not fixed**

We can all develop our intelligence.

‣ **The pupil voice**

We should be learning from the pupils.

‣ **Principles that make a difference in learning**

Six general principles that research tells us make a significant difference in learning.

‣ **Multiple intelligences**

Gardner's multiple intelligences.

'Imagination is more important than knowledge. Knowledge is limited. Imagination encircles the world.'

Albert Einstein

Effective Teachers in Primary Schools

This section aims to give a flavour of some of the factors that teachers might consider in endeavouring to become more effective classroom practitioners. These suggestions should serve as a stimulus for more in-depth reading. I am in no way implying that there is one right way to go about the complex process of teaching. Recent research would suggest that the following things are important to consider.

The Kolb cycle

In 1998, Blasé and Blasé wrote that:

Studies of innovation show that sustained improvement in teaching often hinges on the development of 'teachers as learners' who collaborate with one another to study teaching and its effects.

If this is indeed the case then it follows that it is important for us all as teachers to understand how we ourselves learn. Kolb (Honey and Munford, 1986) suggested that when an individual is learning, he or she tends to go through a cycle involving:

▸ **concrete experience** – in the Kolb cycle, concrete experience refers to experiencing the world through our senses

▸ **reflective observation** – to learn from the concrete experience, we must reflect in a conscious way on what we have learned

▸ **abstract conceptualization** – to make sense of what we have experienced, we must now relate the new information to existing meaning structures we possess, and through this we move to a state of a new meaning and understanding

▸ **active experimentation** – we then test our new meaning and understanding by taking further action or experimentation, which again leads to new experience.

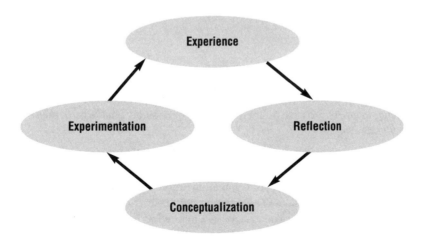

According to Kolb, different people become more efficient in performing different stages of this cyclic process, and in this way each person develops a preferred learning style.

Although it is possible to enter the cycle at any stage, for the learning to become embedded the full sequence should be experienced.

In teaching, the process of reflection is of vital importance. It is how the things we do on a daily basis, and the skills, knowledge and talents we employ to do them, can move from the unconscious to the conscious level. Improvement can take place when we become more consciously aware of what we do, how we do it and why we do it. We can then work on certain areas of apparent weakness and develop the undoubted strengths we also have. It would be worthwhile for all of us to spend some time considering how we learn.

Unconscious learning

A great deal of what we learn in teaching operates on the unconscious level. We take in experiences through our lives as teachers and these greatly influence what we do without our sometimes being aware of it. The same is true when we are watching the teachers in the VITAL videos. A lot of the learning process will operate on the subconscious level. It has been suggested (Norretranders, 1998) that the data-handling capability of the unconscious to the conscious is in a ratio of one million to one. A good example of the work of the subconscious is as follows. We have all probably experienced the frustration of battling with a problem that seemed to offer no potential solution. In sheer desperation, we might decide to take a break, leaving the problem behind until another suitable time. This is often when the subconscious data handling comes forward and presents the solution we had previously fought so hard with our conscious mind to uncover.

Most of our learning may, then, take place through the unconscious. However, it is generally accepted that it is important for us to become consciously aware of what we do and why we do it so that we can make conscious decisions about ways in which we can adapt, modify and build on what we do well, while at the same time moving towards a level of competence in those areas that are not our dominant strengths.

Reflective writing

One way of bridging the gap and moving from unconscious to conscious competence is to employ reflective writing about our teaching or about our observations of others' teaching. This can help to tap into the unconscious and make sense of the things we sometimes do without being aware of why we do them. It will progressively enable us to move towards a state of *conscious competence*.

The process of reflective writing can be structured in a number of ways to help people arrive at a state of conscious competence. It might start with simple note-taking during an observation period, and then lead on to something more substantial constructed from these notes and subsequent discussions. The writing might be carried out as a solitary activity by the observer, in the first instance at least, or as a joint effort by several observers, or by the observer and the observed teacher. It could be written with a view to presenting it to other staff, or solely as a personal reflection.

Observing colleagues teach, or indeed watching the teachers in the VITAL videos, has enormous benefits that derive mainly from the reflection and discussion such observation provokes. In work carried out by Mervyn Flecknoe (2002), teachers reported that the act of observing colleagues teach can have several advantages.

- ▸ It enables observational data about incidents in the classroom to be fed back to the observed teacher – for instance, the number of times boys and girls are asked to contribute, the covert behaviour of members of the class as observed by the visitor – and these data are often valuable insights for the observed teacher.

- ▸ It enables praise and admiration to be given within a profession that is used to accepting blame and criticism.

- ▸ It can act as the starting point for discussion about better ways to teach and how to facilitate learning.

However, Flecknoe says that the principal benefit of lesson observations may well be to the observer, who is given the opportunity to reflect upon his or her own teaching while observing another teacher coping with the same or similar situations. As I have indicated, I believe that this can also be one of the real benefits of looking at the teachers in the VITAL videos.

After studying the teachers featured in this resource, or observing teachers in their own school, certain teachers may arrive at the conclusion that they are more or less happy with their own classroom practice. Going through a reflective process and arriving at a level of conscious competence, however, is the main purpose of observing and studying other teachers in action. Using reflective writing as part of this process is a powerful tool that can greatly enhance the conscious understanding of a teacher about the very complex nature of what goes on in a classroom.

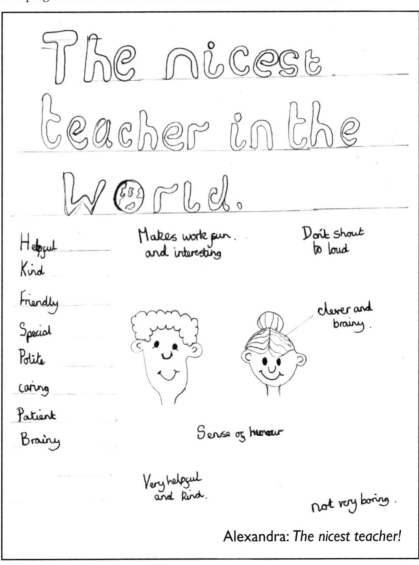

Alexandra: *The nicest teacher!*

Moving towards a common language and research

To be consciously competent practitioners as teachers, and to be able to share our understanding with others, we need to use a common language that assists the transfer of ideas. This can start to develop when teachers engage in a discussion about teaching.

Busher, Harris and co-workers (2000) say:

> Many teachers are excellent practitioners but are unable to describe this practice with any precision. This tacit knowledge is implicit in the practice of all teachers but when teachers are encouraged to articulate and explain their practice this has a powerful effect on their professional learning.

Teachers know this already from the subject or subjects they teach. What they thought that they had 'learned' can appear to be very vague once they start teaching it to a class. There is an old adage in teaching that says that you have never really understood something until you have taught it. In a similar way, what we may instinctively feel we understand about the process of teaching will improve significantly once we start to articulate our ideas through a dialogue with each other about teaching.

Clearly, this articulation can occur when teachers discuss their practice together, but it can also occur when they employ reflective writing. This can be a source of real enjoyment (fun, dare I say!) once the process is started.

Flecknoe again writes that:

> What managers in education can do is to stop putting in place obstacles to self-development. Teachers need to be encouraged into mutual observation rather than frightened off it by inspection; they need opportunities to discuss with colleagues while co-professionals and pupils do the administration; they need encouragement to take risks with pupil voice; they need access to books, journals, and, dare I say it, to university professional development opportunities.

I am confident that most teachers would entirely agree with this sentiment. To be fair, there have been several initiatives designed to stimulate teacher research and a sense of reflection on classroom practice.

Research can provide a variety of benefits, which include an impact on the self-efficacy of teachers, making them feel more valued and more able to influence the future of education. Philippa Cordingley, Chief Executive of CUREE (the Centre for the Use of Research and Evidence in Education), speaks very positively about the present situation concerning educational research in England. She says:

> If the rapid development of interest and involvement in systematic learning is a test of a healthy education system, then I think teachers in England and those who support them are fitter than we might suppose.

She also adds that:

> *I am optimistic that engagement with and in research is part of the solution to the crisis of teacher morale and professional self-esteem.*

If this is indeed the case, then every leader in every school should be actively encouraging teachers to participate in research. I know that this is now happening in many schools – the aim should be for it to be the norm in all schools.

Research in education is meant to benefit teachers and pupils. The trouble is that teachers often underestimate their own skills and what they can offer to the profession. The VITAL project resources will, hopefully, give some insight into the tremendous expertise that already exists in our schools and that can be used and developed for the future of teaching and learning in our classrooms.

Emotional intelligence

In recent times, the part that emotional intelligence can play in the life success of individuals has become a popular theme in education. This has raised awareness that, while good cognitive abilities and technical skills are important, what really matters is our level of emotional intelligence. Learning has to do with *wanting* to make sense of something. So the whole brain, including the emotions, has to be involved. You simply cannot separate emotions from intellect if effective learning is to be achieved.

An understanding of emotional intelligence is as important for us as individuals as it is for the pupils we teach. Daniel Goleman's best-selling book *Emotional Intelligence* (1996) describes how occupational success depends on so many things beyond those that are normally tested. These include self-awareness, self-regulation, motivation, empathy and social skills. These qualities are clearly of vital importance in today's world and yet they are difficult to assess in schools and therefore can be potentially thought of as less important in the target-setting and result-dominated educational society in which we live. It is very difficult for individual schools to change this, of course, when educational qualifications are now seen worldwide as a passport to occupational success. In addition, Goleman (1999) points out that there is a real problem with the structures traditionally employed for education because the emotional brain learns in a different way from the rational brain – so, while a classroom setting may be appropriate for learning technical skills, it is almost useless for learning to behave in a more emotionally intelligent way.

Patricia Broadfoot, in the BERA Stenhouse Lecture in 1999, said:

> *If we accept, as the research suggests, that learning is learnable, multifarious and as much emotional as intellectual, and that self-knowledge and self-esteem are central to it, then our first priority as teachers and policy-makers has to be the creation of an appropriate personal and social setting for learning.*

If the ultimate success of an individual depends so much on their emotional intelligence, as it is sometimes called, then teachers would be wise to study ways of positively influencing this. Daniel Goleman's *Emotional Intelligence* is a useful starting point in consideration of this.

Intelligence is not fixed

Psychological research concerning intelligence reveals not only that there are 'multiple intelligences' (in Howard Gardner's words), but that 'intelligence' is also not a fixed commodity. Research indicates, for example, that:

▶ IQ test scores have been rising in recent years

▶ IQ levels tend to rise or fall depending on individual circumstances

▶ IQ levels tend to be affected by the cultural environment – that is, how people live, what they value and what they do.

The importance of setting the right kind of classroom environment is critical in allowing pupils to develop their learning skills and intellects. To help achieve this, effective teachers will tend to reduce stress and anxiety in the classroom, for example. Brain research indicates that stress and anxiety directly oppose effective learning. The term 'downshifting' describes how, if the brain experiences either threat or fear, it will tend to move to the primitive state of preparation for 'fight or flight', where learning becomes increasingly difficult.

The pupil voice

Taking on board the views of pupils, and involving them in their learning, is crucial in school improvement. This is something that we should perhaps all consider, to become more effective as teachers. Pickering (1997) suggested six reasons why pupils' views and involvement are essential.

1 Pupils need to be at the centre of their learning, to increase motivation and educational productivity.

2 Pupils are valuable for the feedback they can give about their learning.

3 Pupils need to be included in the debate about their learning because it is *their* learning.

4 Pupils can be powerful partners in school improvement as co-researchers.

5 Pupils should be involved in responsible debate about their education, because this reflects the level of responsibility that many have in their lives outside school.

6 Schools must work with pupils and reflect their work.

The ways in which individual schools and teachers go about seeking pupils' views could be very different.

At one level, 'year council' groups can provide valuable feedback. In addition, a whole range of commercial surveys and questionnaires are available today, which can also be valuable. Alternatively, schools may decide to adopt their own approach to gathering the views of pupils, which may involve a variety of methods. However it is done, the important thing is that pupils should feel and know that their views and ideas actually influence the education they receive in school.

Principles that make a difference in learning

I have already stated that I believe that implicit in the notion of effective teaching is effective learning. An effective teacher will always be conscious of the level of learning that is taking place in his or her classroom. There are, however, certain factors that should be considered in terms of providing the right setting or environment for effective learning to take place. From their studies, Ruddock, Chaplin and co-workers (1996) set out the following principles:

1 respect for pupils as individuals and as a body occupying a significant position in the institution of the school

2 fairness to all pupils irrespective of their class, gender, ethnicity or academic status

3 autonomy – not as an absolute state but as both a right and a responsibility in relation to physical and social maturity

4 intellectual challenge that helps pupils to experience learning as a dynamic, engaging and empowering activity

5 social support in relation to both academic and emotional concerns

---

6 security in relation to both the physical setting of the school and in interpersonal encounters (including anxiety about threats to pupils' self-esteem).

Individual teachers and schools could usefully reflect on these principles as a way of assessing whether, in general, effective learning is likely to be taking place.

Multiple intelligences

The various intelligences a human being possesses have been described in different ways. Sternberg (1985) divided intelligence into the following:

▶ analytic

▶ creative

▶ practical.

Howard Gardner defined intelligence as a biopsychological potential to process information, which can be activated in a cultural setting to solve problems or create products that are of value in that culture.

Taylor: *A super teacher!*

Gardner originally divided the intelligences into the following seven categories (1993):

1 linguistic intelligence

2 logical-mathematical intelligence

3 visual-spatial intelligence

4 musical intelligence

5 interpersonal intelligence

6 intrapersonal intelligence

7 bodily-kinesthetic intelligence.

In fact, recently, Howard Gardner has raised the number of 'multiple intelligences' to 'eight and a half'. The additional intelligences Gardner has now identified are:

8 naturalistic intelligence

9 spiritual intelligence.

Naturalistic intelligence is an ability to classify the environment. More hesitantly, Gardner adds spiritual intelligence as being the ability to raise the big questions such as 'What is going to happen to us?' and 'Why are we here?'

Each of us possesses these intelligences to a certain extent and different intelligences for different people probably act as entry points to engage other intelligences. Gardner's own personal entry point is often music. Many people will also have experienced how a piece of music can act as a catalyst for a train of thought, ideas and memories.

There have been critics of Gardner's work. If there are now 'eight and a half' intelligences, where once there were seven, why can we not define 10, 15 or 20? Gardner argues, however, that there is great value to be had in looking at the multiple intelligences of children in action (2002). He says:

> *Any teacher who's really awake watching kids in the classroom designed to encourage the use of multiple intelligences will learn a lot about how they learn.*

A great deal has already been written about multiple intelligences. This is not the place to describe them in detail, but there are some excellent books available for those who wish to study multiple intelligences further, including *Accelerated Learning in the Classroom* by Alistair Smith (Network Educational Press, 1996) and *The Learning Revolution* by Gordon Dryden and Dr Jeannette Vos (Network Educational Press, 2001). The important thing for teachers is to appreciate that we should all try to develop these intelligences for the pupils we teach. Alistair Smith says that:

> *Work completed by others in the field of Accelerated Learning suggests that the development of a full range of intelligences assists long-term learning in general.*

There is a great deal of overlap between the 'interpersonal' and 'intrapersonal' multiple intelligences and the emotional intelligence referred to earlier on. These things are so important in the development of individuals and their ultimate success in life. As Gardner and others have suggested, IQ tests predict school performance with considerable accuracy but they are only an indifferent predictor of performance in a profession after formal schooling. The way in which an individual can relate to others (their interpersonal intelligence) and their ability to access their own feelings (their intrapersonal intelligence) are crucial in terms of their success once they leave school. These are things that all effective teachers will attempt to strengthen in the pupils they teach.

In some ways, these multiple intelligences can also be thought of as the 'talents' of the individual, which were referred to earlier on. Piaget saw talent and intelligence as being the same thing. He considered it absurd that a person might be able to do some things really very well, but would not be thought 'smart' if those things happened not to be connected to school success.

The natural conclusion to draw from Gardner's view that everyone has a different set of intelligences is that there should be an individualized education system. Indeed, this is what Gardner proposed in a speech in Holland in 2001. This is incredibly radical, and conflicts again with the culture in so many schools at present, based on a fact-laden, centralized education system. However radical, though, it may be one of the ways in which future education in our schools can really take a massive leap forward. Many schools are now spending a lot of time looking at providing personal and individualized learning. Through this we may be at the start of something that can impact significantly on education we provide for everyone in schools.

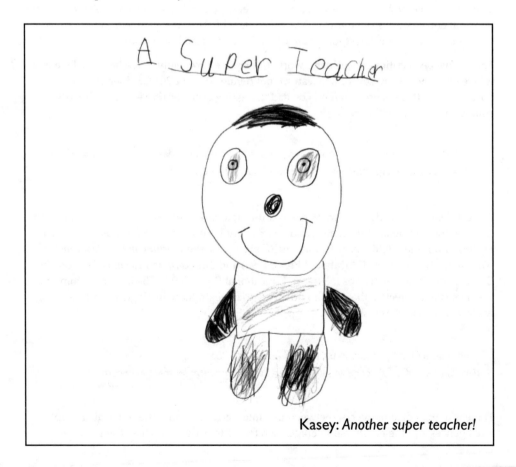

Kasey: *Another super teacher!*

Effective Teachers in Primary Schools

Section 5

The Hay McBer Report as a framework and how to use VITAL

This section concerns the following.

➡ **Using the VITAL materials**

The different ways of using the VITAL materials in this resource.

➡ **The three parts of the Hay McBer Report**

These are Teaching Skills, Professional Characteristics and Classroom Climate.

➡ **Teaching Skills**

The seven Teaching Skills identified by Hay McBer.

➡ **Professional Characteristics**

The 16 characteristics identified, grouped into five clusters.

➡ **Classroom Climate**

The nine dimensions of Classroom Climate.

➡ **Some of the findings from the Hay McBer Report**

Some general words about the findings in the Hay McBer Report and reference to the website.

'I am always ready to learn, but I do not always like being taught.'

Sir Winston Churchill

Using the VITAL materials

VITAL draws heavily on the findings of *A Model of Teacher Effectiveness: Report by Hay McBer to the Department for Education and Employment, June 2000*. The effectiveness of each teacher has therefore been related to the written comments in the Hay McBer Report. Below you will find a summary of the categories within the Hay McBer Report.

There are a number of ways you may wish to use the information in the VITAL materials. For example:

1   You may wish to look at the edited sections on the long video (approximately 20 minutes) for each of the six teachers and draw your own conclusions first. You may then like to compare your analysis with the things I have highlighted about each teacher in Section Six of this book.

2   Alternatively, you may wish to look at the video evidence first, including the short introductory video, read and listen to my comments and then add your own views on what makes each teacher effective.

The VITAL materials can be used:

▸ as a mechanism for discussion during school INSET concerning classroom management

▸ by individual teachers at home who may wish to review their own approach to teaching as all good professionals should do

▸ by ITT and GTP students who may wish to supplement their own classroom observation with examples of effective teachers in other schools

▸ by training colleges who wish to give their classroom students examples of effective teachers and use this as a means of discussion

▸ by teachers who are reflecting on their classroom teaching practice as the approach to their Threshold application

▸ by teachers who are reflecting on their classroom teaching practice as they move through the stages of 'performance management'.

We must all, as teachers, be prepared continually to improve and adopt new methods of teaching and learning. The Hay McBer Report makes this clear:

Effective teachers in the future will need to deal with a climate of continual change.

Schools may wish to use the VITAL materials during INSET days, or individual teachers can view and study them in the comfort of their own homes.

My experience of working on the VITAL project has convinced me that effective teachers are found throughout the whole range of the teaching profession, in both the primary and secondary sectors. Teachers are of all ages with various levels of experience and a range of individual talents. The Hay McBer Report comes to this conclusion too:

We found that biometric data (i.e. information about teachers' age and teaching experience, additional responsibilities, qualifications, career history and so on) did not allow us to predict their effectiveness as a teacher. Effective and outstanding teachers came from diverse backgrounds. Effective and outstanding teachers teach in all kinds of schools and school contexts.

The three parts of the Hay McBer Report

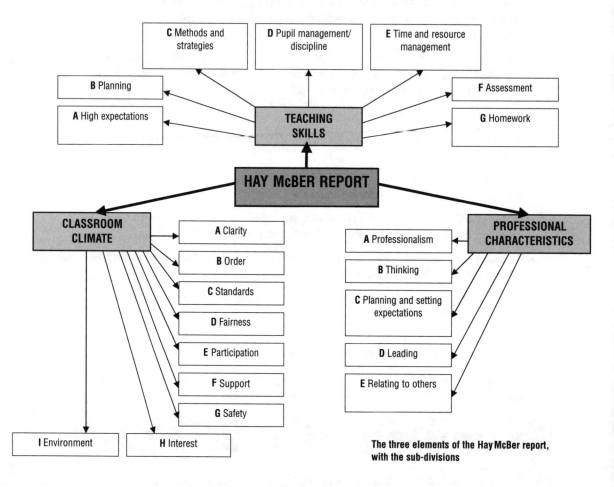

The three elements of the Hay McBer report, with the sub-divisions

A Model of Teacher Effectiveness: Report by Hay McBer to the Department for Education and Employment, June 2000 looks at the effectiveness of teachers by dividing the analysis up into three key elements. These are:

1 Teaching Skills

2 Professional Characteristics

3 Classroom Climate.

All of these things are within teachers' control and, undoubtedly, significantly influence pupil progress. The following looks at the way in which these three elements are further sub-divided.

Teaching Skills

The report sub-divides Teaching Skills into seven categories as follows:

A High expectations

B Planning

C Methods and strategies

D Pupil management/discipline

E Time and resource management

F Assessment

G Homework.

These are similar to the OFSTED inspection headings. In addition, Hay McBer says that Teaching Skills can be observed in terms of:

▸ the way the lesson is structured and flows, and

▸ the number of pupils on task through the course of the lesson.

Professional Characteristics

The report sub-divides Professional Characteristics into five clusters of characteristics as shown below.

Cluster	Characteristics
A Professionalism	II Challenge and support II Confidence II Creating trust II Respect for others
B Thinking	II Analytical thinking II Conceptual thinking
C Planning and setting expectations	II Drive for improvement II Information seeking II Initiative
D Leading	II Flexibility II Holding people accountable II Managing pupils II Passion for learning
E Relating to others	II Impact and influence II Teamworking II Understanding others

Referring to the clusters of Professional Characteristics, the Hay McBer Report says that:

> *Effective teachers need to have some strengths in each of them.*

Recognising the individual nature of each teacher, the report makes clear that:

> *Effective teachers show distinctive combinations of characteristics that create success for their pupils.*

Critically, not all teachers need to be the same. How could we be? The important thing is to strive to develop skills and knowledge that complement our natural talents in such a way that we display a range of Professional Characteristics in each of the clusters shown above.

Classroom Climate

The report sub-divides Classroom Climate into nine dimensions as follows:

A Clarity

Clarity around the purpose of each lesson – how each lesson relates to the broader subject – as well as clarity regarding the aims and objectives of the school.

B Order

Order within the classroom, where discipline, order and civilized behaviour are maintained.

C Standards

A clear set of standards as to how pupils should behave and what each pupil should do and try to achieve, with a clear focus on higher rather than minimum standards.

D Fairness

The degree to which there is an absence of favouritism, and a consistent link between rewards in the classroom and actual performance.

E Participation

The opportunity for pupils to participate actively in the class by discussion, questioning, giving out materials, and other similar activities.

F Support

Pupils should feel emotionally supported in the classroom, so that they are willing to try new things and learn from mistakes.

G Safety

The degree to which the classroom is a safe place, where pupils are not at risk from emotional bullying, or other fear-inducing factors.

H Interest

Pupils should feel that the classroom is an interesting and exciting place to be, where they feel stimulated to learn.

I Environment

Pupils should feel that the classroom is a comfortable, well-organized, clean and attractive physical environment.

Some of the findings from the Hay McBer Report

The Hay McBer Report says that Teaching Skills and Professional Characteristics are factors that relate to what a teacher brings to the job. A distinction between the two factors is drawn as follows:

> *While teaching skills can be learned, sustaining these behaviours over the course of a career will depend on the deeper-seated nature of professional characteristics.*

The report describes the nature of Professional Characteristics in the following way:

> *Professional characteristics are deep-seated patterns of behaviour which outstanding teachers display more often, in more circumstances and to a greater degree of intensity than effective colleagues. They are how the teacher does the job, and have to do with self-image and values; traits, or the way the teacher habitually approaches situations; and at the deepest level, the motivation that drives performance.*

Classroom Climate is referred to as an output measure. Classroom Climate is what the teacher creates through Teaching Skills and Professional Characteristics and it is what influences the pupils to learn.

As already mentioned in Section Three, the Hay McBer Report comfortingly says that teachers are not clones and that there are a number of ways of a teacher achieving effectiveness.

> *There is, in other words, a multiplicity of ways in which particular characteristics determine how a teacher chooses which approach to use from a repertoire of established techniques in order to influence how pupils feel.*

This overview of the Hay McBer Report is useful because in each of the analyses of the teachers in Section Six there are cross references to the factors in the report that match the observed features of the teachers in the videos accompanying this book. Six of the seven Teaching Skills (only excluding 'G Homework') are highlighted in the analyses of the VITAL teachers. All five of the Professional Characteristics clusters, and 15 of the 16 associated characteristics, are highlighted. (The only characteristic not linked with one of the VITAL teachers is 'Understanding others'. I did not attribute this characteristic to any one of the teachers in order that each of the six teachers was linked with three characteristics exactly. In fact, this characteristic can be seen to apply to *all* the VITAL teachers.)

In the analysis of each teacher, I have not referred to the Classroom Climate dimensions because these are what the Hay McBer Report says result from the Teaching Skills and Professional Characteristics. You will no doubt be able to see a number of Classroom Climate dimensions for yourself in each of the lessons shown if you wish to do this. This could indeed be another useful way of using the VITAL materials in this resource.

The following quote from the report indicates that the time has come for us to look at other teachers and the way that they create a favourable classroom climate, while at the same time being open to comments and suggestions about the classroom climate we ourselves create:

> *Despite the demonstrable impact of classroom climate on student motivation and performance, it is rare for British teachers, or teachers in other countries, to receive structured feedback on the climates they help create in their classroom.*

Robin: *Superteach!*

Section 6

An analysis of six teachers

This section concerns the following.

▸▸ **Key Elements**

The use of Key Elements to analyse the six teachers featured in the VITAL videos, and how these are linked to the Teaching Skills and Professional Characteristics described in the Hay McBer Report.

▸▸ **Linking the VITAL teachers with Teaching Skills and Professional Characteristics**

Tables show how the Teaching Skills and Professional Characteristics can be observed in the six VITAL teachers.

▸▸ **Analysis of teacher A: Dale Robinson**

▸▸ **Analysis of teacher B: Alison Stoker**

▸▸ **Analysis of teacher C: Chris Metcalf**

▸▸ **Analysis of teacher D: Anne Henry**

▸▸ **Analysis of teacher E: Mark Wilson**

▸▸ **Analysis of teacher F: Sarah Lancaster**

'Education's purpose is to replace an empty mind with an open one.'

Malcolm Forbes,
American author,
publisher and art collector

Key Elements

'Key Elements' is the term I have used for my own initial thoughts on what I believe makes each of the teachers featured in this resource effective. You might feel that there are other more important elements. In many ways, I hope you do. The process of reflecting and analysing and, as a result, provoking discussion is the most important aspect of teacher observation.

Identifying Key Elements in one teacher does not imply that they do not exist in another. In fact, quite the opposite is true – you will see for yourself when observing the teachers that many of the Key Elements can be seen across a number, if not all, of the teachers filmed. (This is also true of references to the Teaching Skills and Professional Characteristics outlined in the Hay McBer Report and linked here with certain teachers.) Identifying the Key Elements with one particular teacher simply encourages the observer to focus on certain attributes.

You may wish to observe one of the teachers with a colleague, make up your own list of Key Elements, and then compare these with each other. You may then wish, as well, to see how these fit in with the Teaching Skills and Professional Characteristics outlined in the Hay McBer Report, as I have done in the following analysis of each teacher.

Linking the VITAL teachers with Teaching Skills and Professional Characteristics

Teaching Skills

The following list shows how the Hay McBer Teaching Skills can be observed through different teachers in this VITAL resource. 'G Homework' has not been included here. This is not because homework is viewed as unimportant but rather because it is difficult to view this skill in the context of the video evidence in the classroom.

Teaching Skills	VITAL teacher
A High expectations	Sarah Lancaster
B Planning	Mark Wilson
C Methods and strategies	Dale Robinson
D Pupil management/discipline	Alison Stoker
E Time and resource management	Anne Henry
F Assessment	Chris Metcalf

Professional Characteristics

Three Professional Characteristics have been associated with each of the six VITAL teachers. (There are 16 characteristics identified in the Hay McBer Report – linking each teacher with three characteristics has meant that two characteristics have been associated with two teachers, as can be seen overleaf.) This doesn't mean that the teachers do not display the other characteristics – quite the opposite is true, in fact. However, it was felt that linking different characteristics to different teachers made the analysis manageable. It also means that if all the teachers are studied then each of the characteristics can be reflected upon. Alternatively, if the cluster of **A** Professionalism was to be looked at (for example), then the different teachers could be observed within the context of the different characteristics I have linked them with. This is clear from the table below.

Cluster	Characteristics	VITAL teacher
A Professionalism	II Challenge and support	Mark Wilson
	II Confidence	Alison Stoker
	II Creating trust	Chris Metcalf
	II Respect for others	Dale Robinson/Anne Henry
B Thinking	II Analytical thinking	Mark Wilson
	II Conceptual thinking	Alison Stoker/Sarah Lancaster
C Planning and setting expectations	II Drive for improvement	Mark Wilson
	II Information seeking	Anne Henry
	II Initiative	Sarah Lancaster
D Leading	II Flexibility	Alison Stoker
	II Holding people accountable	Chris Metcalf
	II Managing pupils	Sarah Lancaster
	II Passion for learning	Dale Robinson
E Relating to others	II Impact and influence	Dale Robinson
	II Teamworking	Chris Metcalf
	II Understanding others	Anne Henry

Bruce: *Some pupils believe teachers can even fly, apparently!*

Dale Robinson

When you are working with children you've got to leave any baggage behind that you have in your personal life. It's very important that when you are in front of the class you are consistent and very fair. Every child must get an equal opportunity for your time. You must approach each day with the joy of the job.

Dale Robinson – VITAL Teacher Profile

Full Name:	Dale Robinson
Age when filmed:	45
School:	Hutton Rudby Primary School (Yarm)
Number of pupils in the school:	200
Age range:	5–11
Age range Dale has taught:	Year 3, 4, 5, 6
Date Dale joined the school:	January 1989
Years of teaching in total:	23
Previous schools:	Linden Junior School, Countesthorpe (Leicestershire)
Year group taught in the DVD:	Year 6
Number of pupils in this class:	27

Dale Robinson – Key Elements

These are my initial ideas on some of the characteristics that combine to make Dale an effective teacher:

1 a calm approach

2 the pupils have a routine, and know what is expected of them

3 attention to detail

4 specific times for tasks

5 enthusiasm

6 good subject knowledge

7 the use of 'new ideas' in education

8 gentle humour

9 the pupils are encouraged to value the views and efforts of others in the class

10 eye contact and easy, comfortable body language.

Key Element 1 – A calm approach

(Arguably, this is even more important in a primary school teacher than in a secondary teacher – though I am sure that this assertion could provoke very different responses from teachers with perhaps very polarized opinions.)

Dale's gentle and calm approach spreads into the classroom, as I am sure it is clear to see on the video. The pupils feel safe and secure. They have confidence in Dale as the teacher. Dale speaks in a quiet and yet utterly assured fashion to the class. They know he will respect their views and are therefore eager to respond. Dale also encourages further responses from the pupils by always being encouraging and positive when they answer questions.

Key Element 2 – The pupils have a routine, and know what is expected of them

From the very start, the class acts as an entity. (It has always intrigued me how a group of individuals can form a collective identity. Any experienced teacher will have found this, with many of the classes he or she has taught.) There is order and discipline in Dale's classroom and a deep sense of purpose. It is clear that part of this is because the pupils have a set routine and structure for their lessons, which enables them to feel comfortable in knowing what is expected of them.

Key Element 3 – Attention to detail

Pupils do not respond well to generalized praise. A pupil's self-esteem will rise when he or she feels that specific parts of his or her work have been identified and praised. The reason for this is that the pupil will then know that he or she has been closely observed and that the teacher has picked out specific, positive aspects of the work. To use a sporting analogy, 'You played a good game' will not work as well as 'In the second game in the third set, your passing shot down the line to make it 30-all was accurate and exceptional'. Dale also encourages the pupils, through his response to their suggestions, to take their understanding on to an even higher level. He carefully probes in an attempt to achieve excellence.

Key Element 4 – Specific times for tasks

Dale gives the class very specific times to carry out tasks. This encourages them to be more focused and aware of the nature of the task and the structure and progression of the lesson.

Key Element 5 – Enthusiasm

Dale clearly loves teaching. He loves being with the class and this is something all the pupils will sense and respond to. Dale gets a great deal from teaching but this is not just something that happens by chance. Success is a result of a variety of factors, as the VITAL project aims to show. Dedication and hard work are part of the complex mix that enables teachers to achieve success and, as a result, feel fulfilled in their work.

Key Element 6 – Good subject knowledge

Primary school teachers are expected to have a very broad knowledge. Teachers know how important it is to feel comfortable with the subjects they are teaching – it instils yet further confidence in the pupils. Dale clearly demands a lot of the class in terms of the level of language used and the sentence structures. Adverbs, adjectives, similes, metaphors and personification are all worked on in this lesson.

Key Element 7 – The use of 'new ideas' in education

Some people may argue that there are no new ideas in education and that things such as 'accelerated learning' are merely identifying good practice. This may or may not be the case. What is clear, however, is that many teachers have been enthused by the ideas of those working to improve teaching and learning in schools. Dale used the ideas of visualization and playing music to great effect. The class responds well to these techniques, without showing any signs of being uncomfortable or embarrassed. This is quite a feat, but Dale demonstrates that it is perfectly manageable and achievable.

Key Element 8 – Gentle humour

Dale comments on the use of humour in lessons. Humour helps to break potential tension and it also allows pupils to see a side to the teacher that they can enjoy. A teacher who demonstrates humour looks comfortable in what he or she is doing in the classroom. The teacher who is relaxed and enjoying the work will encourage pupils, in a similar way, to relax and enjoy themselves.

Key Element 9 – The pupils are encouraged to value the views and efforts of others in the class

This is very evident when Dale elicits positive responses (feedback) from the class after a child has read out a piece of work. The children also clap spontaneously to show their appreciation of the efforts of another pupil. Each individual shows respect for all other members of the class. This is something that all teachers would probably place at the top of a list of essentials in the classroom.

Key Element 10 – Eye contact and easy, comfortable body language

Along with the quiet and calm way Dale speaks to the class, he demonstrates confidence through his eye contact with the pupils and his relaxed body language. Pupils cannot learn when they feel threatened. A state of relaxed alertness is the ideal state. When the teacher looks relaxed, the pupils will also feel relaxed and comfortable.

Dale Robinson – direct links with the Hay McBer Report

The following describes the links I have made between Dale's teaching and the Hay McBer Report. As for all the teachers, I have chosen one Teaching Skill and three Professional Characteristics.

Teaching Skill

The Teaching Skill from the Hay McBer Report that I have chosen to link Dale with is:

C Methods and strategies.

Two of eight key questions the Hay McBer Report asks about 'methods and strategies' are:

> ▸ *Does the teacher involve all pupils in the lesson?*
>
> ▸ *Does the teacher use a variety of activities/learning methods?*

Watching Dale teach, it is very clear that he involves all the pupils in the lesson and he employs a number of interesting activities (including visualization techniques) to fully engage the pupils in their learning. The Hay McBer Report points out that:

> *Individual work and small group activities were regularly employed as ways of reinforcing pupil learning through practice and reflection.*

We see this in Dale's classroom. In addition the Hay McBer Report says:

> *In our observations we saw effective teachers doing a great deal of active teaching. Many of the activities were led by the teacher. The teachers presented information to the pupils with a high degree of clarity and enthusiasm and, when giving basic instruction, the lessons proceeded at a brisk pace.*

Again, this is evident in Dale's lesson with his clear presentation of the task and attention to detail providing the stimulus for the imaginative work the pupils carry out.

Professional Characteristics

The three Professional Characteristics from the Hay McBer Report that I have chosen to link Dale with are shown below.

Cluster	Characteristics
A Professionalism **D** Leading **E** Relating to others	**II** Respect for others **II** Passion for learning **II** Impact and influence

A Professionalism – Respect for others

(Also see Anne Henry for this Professional Characteristic.) Under Professional Characteristics, and within the cluster of **A** Professionalism, the Hay McBer Report emphasizes the importance of *respect for others*. The report states that:

Listening to others and valuing their contribution is fundamental to the empathy and exchange that is at the heart of education and learning. Effective teachers demonstrate that they respect and value others, so that pupils do the same and are encouraged to share their experiences and insights.

Teachers, when they explicitly value others, shape pupils' and colleagues' perceptions of themselves. This helps them to recognize their unique talents, to feel special, and to have the confidence to succeed. It increases the motivation in all to achieve more than they ever thought they could.

When teachers show that they respect others, it becomes more likely that people throughout the school community will learn from others with diverse backgrounds, and learn to be good citizens.

Showing respect for pupils is perhaps, to me, the most fundamental characteristic of an effective teacher. Dale demonstrates this in a number of ways. He listens carefully to the responses of the pupils, valuing each of their contributions. The children also show great respect for one another, demonstrating an appreciation of the effort each individual makes. Dale will have worked on this over the time he has known the class so that it eventually becomes a natural part of how they operate. They will clearly learn a great deal as they go through their education in schools, but perhaps no single thing will be as important as the understanding that respect for the individual is vital. They are guided and led in this by the words and actions of their teacher, each and every day.

The Key Elements identified earlier that exemplify the way in which Dale shows respect for others include:

▸ the pupils are encouraged to value the views and efforts of others in the class.

D Leading – Passion for learning

Under Professional Characteristics, and within the cluster of **D** Leading, the Hay McBer Report emphasizes the importance of *passion for learning*. The report states that:

> *Having a deep drive to help pupils learn, and to develop a repertoire of learning skills and strategies, means the emphasis and endeavour in the classroom is targeted on pupils' learning development. The degree of energy behind this characteristic is significant in ensuring that every pupil is supported in his or her learning.*

Effective teaching to enable learning at the basic level is about providing a rich learning environment to begin with, which accesses and appeals to the different ways pupils learn. Clear explanations and demonstrations are used to introduce new material and ideas to pupils, and to help them see the standards they should be aiming for in their work.

Supported practice – guidance for pupils as they explore new content, or skills and approaches – is key, so that pupils can try things out for themselves and embed learning. Effectiveness at this level is about successfully *differentiating* and layering teaching, so *all* pupils have an opportunity to progress. Enabling *all* pupils to progress, or to make leaps and bounds in their learning, and consolidate and internalize concepts at a deep level, is a further level of sophistication. It matters because it progressively builds a basis for broad and deep understanding by the pupil.

Dale is constantly learning – an essential characteristic of all effective teachers. This is demonstrated clearly by the way in which Dale embraces the ideas of 'accelerated learning', for example, and is prepared to use these in the classroom. He transmits his passion for learning to the class in a very gentle but persuasive way. Dale encourages the pupils to think for themselves and seeks in the lesson shown on the video to deepen their understanding of complex aspects of literature. The pupils are practising independent learning skills, which will enable them to become lifelong learners, able to respond positively to the challenges of a rapidly changing world.

The Key Elements identified earlier that exemplify the way in which Dale shows a passion for learning include:

- ▸ enthusiasm
- ▸ good subject knowledge
- ▸ the use of 'new ideas' in education.

E Relating to others – Impact and influence
Under Professional Characteristics, and within the cluster of **E** Relating to others, the Hay McBer Report emphasizes the importance of *impact and influence*. The report states that:

> *Influencing is fundamental to creating an environment where pupils feel motivated to learn. It enhances engagement with learning. It is needed to make learning vivid and fun, and to create not just memorable lessons but also memorable years for pupils.*

Enthusiasm for a subject or specialism drives teachers to encourage pupils to share their passion for it. Consequently, they will find ways to put it across in an appealing way. Effective teachers calculate lesson content so that it is intellectually stimulating and challenging, as well as offering plenty of variety, so that pupils enjoy learning and want to be there.

The ability to influence is also important when pupils are finding the going tough, when they experience a setback, or when they are flagging. Here creativity really helps; and having a range of teaching techniques and knowing when to use them is critical. It is critical for all teachers, particularly those in leadership roles, to be able to influence others. To do this, they draw on an understanding of, and sensitivity to, the politics of the school. Successful influencing is particularly important in dealing with parents. It is also critical in influencing colleagues to work together in achieving optimal learning outcomes.

It is hard to say for certain at this stage what long-term impact and influence Dale will have on the pupils he teaches. I dare say, however, that it will be significant. The techniques he successfully uses with the class will be something they will remember and be able to use themselves. In addition, I believe it is true to say that Dale's deep understanding and enthusiasm for the work he does with the class will have a strong influence on how they engage with learning in the future.

The Key Elements identified earlier that exemplify the way in which Dale has an impact and influence include:

- enthusiasm
- good subject knowledge
- the use of 'new ideas' in education
- the pupils are encouraged to value the views and efforts of others in the class.

This table shows the teaching skill and professional characteristics identified in the analysis of Dale.

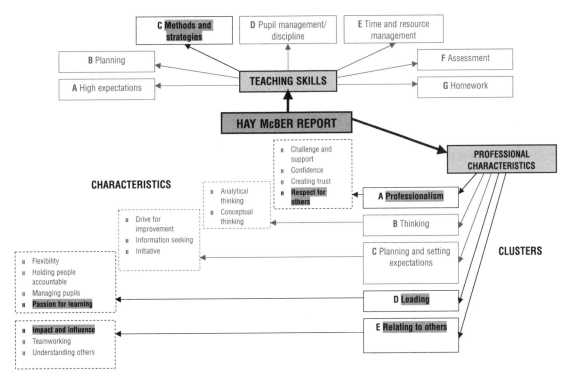

DALE ROBINSON – Teaching Skills and Professional Characteristics identified in the analysis

Alison Stoker

It's vital that teachers should recognize that there is never one way that is the right way and that we can all learn something from watching other people. No matter how small, there are all sorts of tips and techniques that other people use that would help us to be better, more effective and understanding teachers.

Alison Stoker – VITAL Teacher Profile

Full Name:	Alison Stoker
Age when filmed:	44
School:	Little London Community Primary School (Leeds)
Number of pupils in the school:	216
Age range:	4–11
Age range Alison has taught:	I currently teach ICT to every age group from nursery to year 6. I have also taught Year 3, 4, 5, and 6 as a class teacher.
Date Alison joined the school:	April 1997
Years of teaching in total:	7
Previous schools:	Various supply work
	Tadcaster East Primary (North Yorkshire)
	Athelston Primary (North Yorkshire)
	Parklands Primary School (Leeds)
Year group taught in the DVD:	Year 6
Number of pupils in this class:	25

Alison Stoker – Key Elements

These are my initial ideas on some of the characteristics that combine to make Alison an effective teacher:

1 using ICT in the classroom

2 an undercurrent of humour

3 relating lessons to the experiences of pupils

4 learning by playing

5 pupils make contributions

6 voice and position

7 use of names

8 smile

9 enthusiasm.

Key Element 1 – Using ICT in the classroom

ICT now plays an important part in lessons in both secondary and primary schools. Pupils can be really motivated by lessons involving computers. Teachers need to be competent themselves in the use of ICT. Alison is clearly both comfortable and confident in using computers as an educational tool. Part of the work Alison does in the school, in fact, is to train other teachers in how to use ICT in their classrooms.

Key Element 2 – An undercurrent of humour

Humour was mentioned as a tool in the analysis of Dale's lesson. Alison has a very different approach to using humour but the effect is very similar. Pupils are made to feel relaxed in the presence of a teacher who seems to be enjoying what she is doing. The children receive the message that their teacher is happy to be with them.

Humour is an essential tool in the teacher toolbox.

Key Element 3 – Relating lessons to the experiences of pupils

Here, Alison bases the lesson (dealing with spreadsheets) around buying and selling footballers. Most of the children would be interested in this, particularly given that when this lesson was filmed the World Cup was about to start. A lesson based on the interests and experiences of the pupils will tend to flow and have more interest and relevance for the class.

Key Element 4 – Learning by playing

Pupils can sometimes learn best when they don't think they are learning – when they think that what they are doing is just good fun. The lesson here is designed in such a way that the pupils think they are playing a game – with a little bit of competition involved to give an extra edge to it.

Key Element 5 – Pupils make contributions

Alison constantly invites pupils to contribute to the lesson by, for example, coming out to the front and operating the Smartboard. They can then be seen instantly by the rest of the class. They also receive the message that their expertize and ideas are valued.

Key Element 6 – Voice and position

Alison deliberately takes up a central position in the classroom. The pupils know that when Alison is talking from here they must listen. She also speaks in a clear way such that pupils can pick up her messages even when they are involved in their own work. When she is not in this central position, she is active in helping pupils with their individual learning.

Key Element 7 – Use of names

Alison constantly uses the names of the pupils. Children, like adults, are sensitive about their names. Using a child's name will instantly make him or her feel identified and known by the teacher. It makes the child feel valued as an individual.

Key Element 8 – Smile

Smiling is another tool that many teachers use without sometimes thinking about it. It can say so much, including:

- ▸ 'I am confident'
- ▸ 'I am happy to be with you'
- ▸ 'I expect you to be happy as well'.

Smiling can have a really positive effect on the behaviour of pupils and the atmosphere in a classroom. In a similar way to humour, a smile can bring warmth and a relaxed approach to learning.

Key Element 9 – Enthusiasm

Alison shows, by her enthusiastic manner, that she is interested in what she is doing. This will be picked up by the pupils, who will respond positively. Through Alison's enthusiasm, the pupils will sense her love of learning and, again, her enjoyment in being with them.

Alison Stoker – direct links with the Hay McBer Report

The following describes the links I have made between Alison's teaching and the Hay McBer Report. As for all the teachers, I have chosen one Teaching Skill and three Professional Characteristics.

Teaching Skill

The Teaching Skill from the Hay McBer Report that I have chosen to link Alison with is:

D Pupil management/discipline.

Two of five key questions the Hay McBer Report asks about 'pupil management/discipline' are:

> ▶ *Does the teacher keep the pupils on task throughout the lesson?*
>
> ▶ *Does the teacher praise good achievement and effort?*

Throughout the course of Alison's lesson, we see the class involved in the spreadsheet task of buying footballers. Alison is constantly rewarding the group with praise for their work. The Hay McBer Report goes on to say:

> *Effective teachers have a clear strategy for pupil management. A sense of order prevails in the classroom. Pupils feel safe and secure. This pupil management strategy is a means to an end: allowing maximum time for pupils to be focused on the task, and thus maximising the learning opportunity. Effective teachers establish and communicate clear boundaries for pupil behaviour. They exercise authority clearly and fairly from the outset, and in their styles of presentation and engagement they hold the pupils' attention. Inappropriate behaviour is 'nipped in the bud' with immediate direct action from the teacher.*

Within any group, children will come to school from a variety of backgrounds and it is important that they should feel secure in the classroom. Alison provides that security and shows by her relaxed manner, including smiling and the use of humour, that she is in control of the group.

In addition the Hay McBer Report says:

> *Some effective teachers employ a 'catch them being good' policy whereby pupil behaviour which is appropriate and on task is recognised and reinforced by praise. One outstanding teacher referred to the importance of the 'lighthouse effect' – being fully aware of everything that is going on in the classroom and having 360° vision.*

The complexity of any classroom environment is demonstrated when we look at Alison's lesson. A teacher needs to be fully aware of what is going on around him or her, while at the same time addressing the needs of an individual. Mastering the 'lighthouse effect' is very important.

Professional Characteristics

The three Professional Characteristics from the Hay McBer Report that I have chosen to link Alison with are shown below.

Cluster	Characteristics
A Professionalism	**II** Confidence
B Thinking	**II** Conceptual thinking
D Leading	**II** Flexibility

A Professionalism – Confidence

Under Professional Characteristics, and within the cluster of **A** Professionalism, the Hay McBer Report emphasizes the importance of *confidence*. The report states that:

> *Effective teachers believe in themselves and have the conviction to be ambitious: for their pupils, for the school, and for themselves.*
>
> *Confidence for many teaching practitioners stems from experience. It readily communicates itself to others. It builds the optimism needed to try things out, to aim high, and to succeed. Self-confidence is also fundamental to challenging poor performance and bringing about step change.*
>
> *Effective teachers see themselves as, and act as, 'leading professionals'. They have the emotional resilience to deal with challenging pupils, and the stamina necessary for a sustained contribution in the classroom.*
>
> *Being confident about personal skills and believing in the value of their work in what they know is a demanding job, helps teachers to have a strong sense of identity, and to set boundaries for themselves so they know what they can and should take on.*

Alison displays great confidence in the lesson she leads. There is an implicit sense in which she gives the message that she believes what she is doing is important and that the pupils will learn from and enjoy the work they are doing. Alison leads by example. She allows other teachers into her lesson to see the ICT work she is doing with groups so that her expertise can be shared with others. Other teachers can learn by watching, reflecting upon and copying Alison's techniques.

The Key Elements identified earlier that exemplify the way in which Alison shows confidence include:

- ▸ using ICT in the classroom
- ▸ an undercurrent of humour
- ▸ voice and position
- ▸ enthusiasm.

B Thinking – Conceptual thinking

Under Professional Characteristics, and within the cluster of **B** Thinking, the Hay McBer Report emphasizes the importance of *conceptual thinking*. The report states that:

> *Effective teachers develop lessons and programmes of work which deliver the curriculum in such a way that they provide breadth, balance and continuity, and match the level and needs of their classes and the individuals within them. They therefore move easily between the big picture and the detail.*
>
> *They also make links between areas of the curriculum, so that learning can be consolidated across different subjects, and think about connections they see outside the classroom and beyond the school, to enhance and enrich teaching and learning.*
>
> *Pupils will progress if they fully understand concepts and subject content, so the ability to clarify and simplify complex ideas and communicate them is very important.*

In Alison's lesson, the pupils are actively involved in spreadsheet work, which is accessed through something that will be of real interest to many of them – football. They learn by doing, and by doing something that has an inherent interest for them.

The Key Elements identified earlier that exemplify the way in which Alison shows conceptual thinking include:

- relating lessons to the experiences of pupils
- learning by playing
- pupils make contributions.

D Leading – Flexibility

Under Professional Characteristics, and within the cluster of **D** Leading, the Hay McBer Report emphasizes the importance of *flexibility*. The report states that:

> *Getting the best for pupils means being open-minded about new approaches and being prepared to try things out.*
>
> *Pupils in any one class have a range of abilities, and learn in a variety of ways. Effective teachers differentiate their teaching so that all pupils learn in the lesson. This requires teachers to draw on a range of teaching techniques, and match these to the needs of pupils and of the situation.*
>
> *Flexibility is also one way of obtaining value from experiential learning, so that real and unpredictable material, especially that which pupils bring with them into the class, can be used fruitfully.*
>
> *Spontaneity generates vitality in learning, helps to make it enjoyable, and may help the growth of creative and imaginative approaches to problem-solving.*

All teachers need to be flexible. They need to respond to the changing and unexpected demands of a class. Alison listens carefully to the often imaginative suggestions of the class, sometimes wanting to bend the rules of the exercise, and she adds to these her contribution. The best way forward is often through guided instruction and negotiation.

The Key Elements identified earlier that exemplify the way in which Alison shows flexibility include:

- using ICT in the classroom
- learning by playing
- pupils make contributions
- enthusiasm.

This table shows the teaching skill and professional characteristics identified in the analysis of Alison.

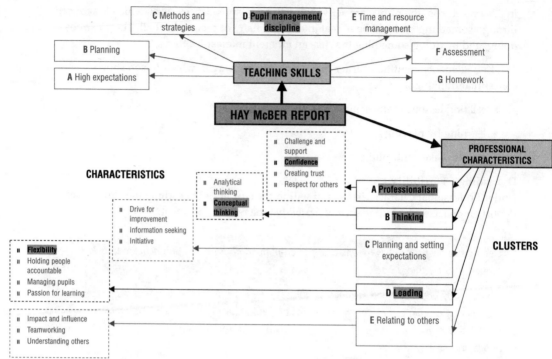

CHARACTERISTICS

CLUSTERS

ALISON STOKER – Teaching Skills and Professional
Characteristics identified in the analysis

Chris Metcalf

I've been teaching for 25 years now and you never stop learning. You learn from experienced teachers, from student and NQT teachers and from all others in the school. I try to remain enthusiastic and welcoming all the time for the children. I think it is really important when they walk through the door each morning that they feel part of what is going on.

Chris Metcalf – VITAL Teacher Profile

Full Name:	Christopher Metcalf
Age when filmed:	47
School:	Horsforth Newlaithes Junior School (Leeds)
Number of pupils in the school:	188
Age range:	7–11
Age range Chris has taught:	5–11
Date Chris joined the school:	September 1988
Years of teaching in total:	25
Previous schools:	Hawksworth Primary School (Leeds)
	St Bartholomew's C of E, Armley (Leeds)
Year group taught in the DVD:	Year 5
Number of pupils in this class:	30

Chris Metcalf – Key Elements

These are my initial ideas on some of the characteristics that combine to make Chris an effective teacher.

1 warmth of personality and soft tone of voice

2 knowing the pupils

3 mutual trust

4 clear lesson structure

5 attention to detail

6 an air of calm, action and individual learning

7 pupils make contributions

8 a focus on nature and the experiences of pupils

9 challenge creating fun

10 a magician and performer.

Key Element 1 – Warmth of personality and soft tone of voice

Chris talks to the class in a calm, quiet voice. This encourages them to listen carefully to what he says. It also makes them feel warm and secure in his presence. Chris is warm and approachable in the way he conducts himself in the classroom. None of this hides the authority he has with all the pupils.

Key Element 2 – Knowing the pupils

In all his dealings with the class, Chris demonstrates that he knows the children very well. He takes interest in them, asking questions about their own interests and views.

Key Element 3 – Mutual trust

Chris has the confidence in his teaching to trust the pupils and it is clear that they have trust in him as well. Along with Chris, the pupils own and take pride in their classroom. It is a safe environment where they can express themselves and develop as individuals.

Key Element 4 – Clear lesson structure

Good lessons seem to flow. The Hay McBer Report makes some reference to this. The flow of a lesson, however, does not happen by accident. Chris' lesson flows because he has a clear structure to the activities, which comes as a result of careful planning.

Key Element 5 – Attention to detail

An effective teacher will be sensitive to, and will constantly respond to, the needs of the class as they arise. For example, during the lesson Chris senses a problem that a few of the class are having as they practise the seven-times-table. The immediate help that Chris offers the children sends a clear message to them that he is constantly prepared to attend to the fine detail of the learning needs of the individual and of the group.

Key Element 6 – An air of calm, action and individual learning

It is a joy to see a class working both individually and collectively. Individuals are able to develop and work at their own pace while collectively they help each other. That desired state where there is calm but great activity is displayed in Chris' classroom.

Key Element 7 – Pupils make contributions

Chris tries to involve all members of the class in the lesson in a whole variety of ways. He also rewards them for their contributions using 'team points' or comments like 'Excellent concentration', for example.

Key Element 8 – A focus on nature and the experiences of pupils

Chris uses nature as a way of getting pupils to become interested in a broad range of experiences. The wild garden where we interviewed Chris after the lesson was developed by him as a learning environment for the pupils. In addition, he asks the pupils to bring in newspapers for the ongoing activity on timetables. He also asks one boy 'What do you like on TV, apart from *The Simpsons*?' He is implicitly valuing the pupils' lives and experiences by doing this.

Key Element 9 – Challenge creating fun

Chris uses competition at the beginning of the lesson, where he is asking questions in a fun way to motivate the pupils. Pupils often respond well to being involved in competitions. It brings excitement and purpose and makes learning fun.

Key Element 10 – A magician and performer

Chris demonstrates, in a completely calm and controlled fashion, how it is possible to deal with a whole range of activities in the classroom. A teacher has to deal with a myriad of demands placed on him or her by the pupils. This often involves responding to a request from one pupil while trying to explain some important point to another pupil. Remaining in control is absolutely essential.

Chris Metcalf – direct links with the Hay McBer Report

The following describes the links I have made between Chris' teaching and the Hay McBer Report. As for all the teachers, I have chosen one Teaching Skill and three Professional Characteristics.

Teaching Skill

The Teaching Skill from the Hay McBer Report that I have chosen to link Chris with is:

F Assessment.

Two of five key questions the Hay McBer Report asks about 'assessment' are:

> ▸ *Does the teacher use tests, competitions, etc. to assess understanding?*
>
> ▸ *Does the teacher recognise misconceptions and clear them up?*

Chris uses simple competitive techniques to engage the pupils in their work. It keeps them alert and enables him immediately to assess their understanding. When misconceptions or misunderstandings arise, Chris immediately acts to correct these. The Hay McBer Report makes the importance of this clear as follows:

> *It is evident that effective teachers employ a range of assessment methods and techniques to monitor pupils' understanding of lessons and work. These could be tests, competitions, questioning or regular marking of written work.*

In addition, the Hay McBer Report says:

> *The effective teachers look for gains in learning, gaps in knowledge and areas of misunderstanding through their day-to-day work with pupils. Also, effective teachers encourage pupils to judge the success of their own work and to set themselves targets for improvement. They also offer critical and supportive feedback to pupils.*

Professional Characteristics

The three Professional Characteristics from the Hay McBer Report that I have chosen to link Chris with are shown below.

Cluster	Characteristics
A Professionalism	**II** Creating trust
D Leading	**II** Holding people accountable
E Relating to others	**II** Teamworking

A Professionalism – Creating trust

Under Professional Characteristics, and within the cluster of **A** Professionalism, the Hay McBer Report emphasizes the importance of *creating trust*. The report states that:

> *Professional dependability is essential in the school environment where colleagues have to rely on each other. Teachers who show it win pupils' respect and trust, and earn their confidence. Being sincere and genuine creates an atmosphere of trust, and allows pupils to act naturally, express themselves honestly, and not be afraid of making mistakes – an essential starting point for learning. It also helps build rapport with pupils.*
>
> *Strong modelling of this characteristic by teachers, paraprofessionals (for example, non-teaching assistants) and all those involved in the life of the school creates an ethos of mutual trust, and makes the school a dependable point of reference in what for many pupils can seem a turbulent world.*

Effective Teachers in Primary Schools

Chris, like so many teachers, goes way beyond the boundaries of what is needed and expected to bring about an environment for learning in which the pupils can truly flourish. This not only includes the bright, colourful and friendly classroom environment but also the wildlife garden where we filmed Chris. Chris has an openness and sincerity that enables him to win pupils' respect and trust. Chris creates an atmosphere where pupils can learn from experience in a secure and safe environment.

The Key Elements identified earlier that exemplify the way in which Chris creates trust include:

▸ warmth of personality and soft tone of voice

▸ knowing the pupils

▸ mutual trust

▸ an air of calm, action and individual learning.

D Leading – Holding people accountable

Under Professional Characteristics, and within the cluster of **D** Leading, the Hay McBer Report emphasizes the importance of *holding people accountable*. The report states that:

Stating expectations and defining boundaries are needed in order to focus learning and minimize distraction. Clarifying accountability builds a sense of community with shared norms of behaviour. Clear and predictable routines create safety and security.

Being clear about expectations, and contracting with pupils or colleagues in relation to their behaviour and performance, helps individuals to take responsibility and be accountable for themselves and their actions. It is an essential part of enabling pupils to gain a clear understanding about what return they will get from their efforts, and to appreciate what will and will not happen as a result of the actions they choose to take.

When performance is not up to expectations, effective teachers act quickly and capably to achieve the high standards they set. This means that problems can be addressed while performance is recoverable.

There is a sense of calm and intense activity in Chris' classroom. All teachers know that this does not happen by accident. It takes time, effort and dedication and a real sense of purpose to achieve this. Chris will have worked on the behaviour of the pupils to instil in them a sense of values that will influence their behaviour. The pupils clearly respect Chris' techniques as a teacher and therefore react in a positive way towards him. Chris has made a point of getting to know the pupils very well and this enables him to hold them more accountable for the actions they take. It also allows him to take more meaningful action that can have real impact on the pupils.

The Key Elements identified earlier on that exemplify the way in which Chris holds people accountable include:

▸ knowing the pupils

▸ mutual trust

▸ pupils make contributions.

E Relating to others – Teamworking

Under Professional Characteristics, and within the cluster of **E** Relating to others, the Hay McBer Report emphasizes the importance of *teamworking*. The report states that:

> *Teaching is a demanding job, and co-operation and support help create the positive climate needed for continued success. Asking for others' views is also vital, to build a common commitment to change and for increasing effectiveness. Only in this way can the expertise and creativity of all of those who work in the school be maximized.*
>
> *Teamworking between all school colleagues, including support staff and others in the school community, is necessary to ensure an integrated and coherent approach that makes sense to pupils and facilitates their learning. This enhances the delivery of wider school values, policies and practices.*
>
> *Liaising with parents, carers and colleagues means that teachers are working together in partnership to build up an understanding of the whole child and to promote individual development. This informs the careful planning of learning programmes that reflect pupils' learning in different areas and meet pupils' needs.*
>
> *Effective teachers show that teamworking matters because co-operative effort is important in learning and later life. This sort of modelling conveys the importance and value of belonging to a community and being involved with others.*

What is perhaps not easy to capture on video is the way that Chris has a philosophy that is deeply committed to the notion of working with others in partnership. This includes both his work with colleagues (he mentions this in the interview we recorded) and also the way he views working with pupils. Chris has responsibilities in the school beyond the classroom and he again treats this as a way of enabling him to work with his colleagues on future planning.

The Key Elements identified earlier that exemplify the way in which Chris demonstrates teamworking include:

- ‣ knowing the pupils
- ‣ mutual trust.

This table shows the teaching skill and professional characteristics identified in the analysis of Chris.

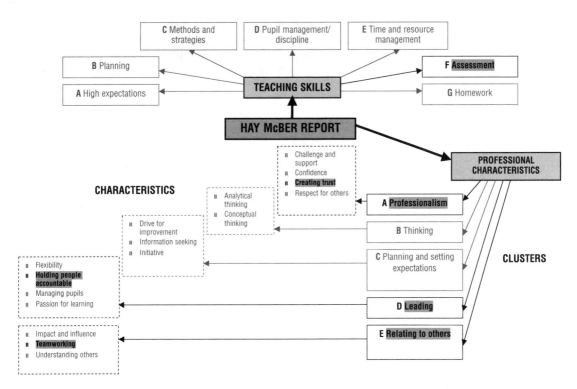

CHRIS METCALF – Teaching Skills and Professional
Characteristics identified in the analysis

Anne Henry

> *I think that more and more as I have experienced lots of different schools I have realized how much I need to change and how much I have "learned" about teaching.*

Anne Henry – VITAL Teacher Profile

Full Name:	Anne Henry
Age when filmed:	53
School:	Darley County Primary School (Harrogate)
Number of pupils in the school:	100
Age range:	5–11
Age range Anne has taught:	Reception and all in KS1 and KS2
Date Anne joined the school:	September 1998
Years of teaching in total:	10 full time and 8 on supply
Previous schools:	Grove Road C P School (Harrogate)
	Oatlands Junior School (Harrogate)
	Dishforth Airfield (North Yorkshire)
	Pannal C P School (Harrogate)
Year group taught in the DVD:	Reception
Number of pupils in this class:	23

Anne Henry – Key Elements

These are my initial ideas on some of the characteristics that combine to make Anne an effective teacher:

1 classroom environment

2 VAK input

3 management of resources

4 the use of Classroom Support Assistants

5 a warm approach that signals care

6 energy, enthusiasm and patience – the eternal optimist!

7 making learning fun

8 being a reflective practitioner.

Key Element 1 – Classroom environment

Crucial to all primary school teachers is the quality of the classroom environment. The delightful colour and range of displays in primary classrooms is something that always impresses me. It is true to say that many secondary school classrooms are also like this (see, for example, the wonderful use of displays by Larraine Biscombe in *Effective Teachers* – the materials from the first stage of the VITAL project). Nevertheless, the displays of primary school classrooms are often particularly wonderful and, as a secondary school teacher myself, I believe there is much to be learned from this particular aspect of primary school classroom management. Anne's classroom is full of life – some of this cannot easily be captured on video. One corner of the room even acts as a 'jungle', which the pupils enter to carry out certain work. This acts as a mechanism to really engage their imaginations.

The classroom environment has such an important impact upon how comfortable and safe pupils will feel. With their own work displayed, they will also experience a sense of ownership.

Key Element 2 – VAK input

Anne deliberately uses a range of Visual, Auditory and Kinesthetic methods to involve the pupils. Her hand movements, for example, have now become part of what the pupils expect from her in her communication with them. She told me that if she does not use these in a lesson the pupils now ask her to do so.

Key Element 3 – Management of resources

Chris Watkins (2000), in a report published by the University of London's Institute of Education, says:

> *The classroom is the most complex and least understood situation on the face of the planet.*

Teaching is a highly complex activity. Most teachers will have experienced the sense of it 'all falling apart' when, for whatever reason, the plan they have for a lesson has to be changed or simply doesn't work. This could be due to late organizational changes suddenly impinging on the teacher's plans. Given that this is the case, it is absolutely essential for a teacher to feel that he or she has all the resources needed for a lesson readily available before the lesson starts. Anne manages this extremely well. All aspects of what she needs for each section of the lesson are in the classroom.

Key Element 4 – The use of Classroom Support Assistants

'Another pair of hands' may be one description of the way in which Classroom Support Assistants can help teachers – and the way in which they can relieve some of the stress of the classroom by assisting with the sheer logistics is very important indeed. But CSAs fulfil a far greater role than this. They can, very ably, assist pupils with their learning and this is what we see in Anne's class.

Key Element 5 – A warm approach that signals care

Young children – in fact, all pupils – tend to respond most positively and learn most effectively when the teacher in front of them is a friendly, approachable figure. It is well known now from research that an individual cannot learn when he or she is feeling threatened. When some form of threat is perceived, the brain will tend to revert to its primitive state of preparation for 'flight or fight', and learning becomes impossible.

Key Element 6 – Energy, enthusiasm and patience – the eternal optimist!

Those who criticize teachers need to experience a few days in the classroom. Teaching requires an abundance of energy and enthusiasm along with all the other skills and characteristics described in the VITAL resources. To first survive and then to develop, teachers have got to learn how to pace themselves throughout the course of each day so that their energy can be directed to where it is most effective. Pupils demand a lot of a classroom teacher. They often don't respond in the way we would like them to. Patience is needed then, so that the situation is under the control of the teacher at all times.

Key Element 7 – Making learning fun

There is little doubt that pupils respond best when they see the learning as being fun. Anne uses a puppet along with beads and planting seeds to bring variety and fun to the lesson.

Key Element 8 – Being a reflective practitioner

I have emphasized in this book the importance of becoming a reflective practitioner. Anne is an experienced teacher who still feels she is learning about the very complex nature of teaching and learning. Important in this is the fact that she does feel she can learn from others and that teaching is not something you are simply blessed with the ability to do. (See Anne's statement at the start of her section in this book.)

Anne Henry – direct links with the Hay McBer Report

The following describes the links I have made between Anne's teaching and the Hay McBer Report. As for all the teachers, I have chosen one Teaching Skill and three Professional Characteristics.

Teaching Skill

The Teaching Skill from the Hay McBer Report that I have chosen to link Anne with is:

E   Time and resource management.

Two of five key questions the Hay McBer Report asks about 'time and resource management' are:

> ‣ *Does the teacher structure the lesson to use the time available well?*
>
> ‣ *Are appropriate learning resources used to enhance pupils' opportunities?*

It is clear from watching Anne teach her lesson that a great deal of planning has gone into achieving something that is smooth-running and effective. The Hay McBer Report says that:

> *The effective management of pupils, time, resources and support promotes good behaviour and effective learning. Effective teachers achieve the management of the class by having a clear structure for each lesson, making full use of planned time, using a brisk pace and allocating his/her time fairly among pupils.*

We see this in Anne's lesson in the way that there are well-defined, structured elements to the lesson that add to make a coherent whole.

In addition, the Hay McBer Report says:

> *In those schools where support and/or parental help was available, the effective teachers involved helpers in the lesson planning stage and in the execution of the lessons. In some instances, support staff were trained in aspects of pupil management, reading support and computer skills.*

Again all pupils in Anne's lesson are catered for, with the Classroom Support Assistant providing help for small groups of pupils.

Professional Characteristics

The three Professional Characteristics from the Hay McBer Report that I have chosen to link Anne with are shown below.

Cluster	Characteristics
A Professionalism	**II** Respect for others
C Planning and setting expectations	**II** Information seeking
E Relating to others	**II** Understanding others

A Professionalism – Respect for others

(Also see Dale Robinson for this Professional Characteristic.) Under Professional Characteristics, and within the cluster of **A** Professionalism, the Hay McBer Report emphasizes the importance of *respect for others*. The report states that:

> *Listening to others and valuing their contribution is fundamental to the empathy and exchange that is at the heart of education and learning. Effective teachers demonstrate that they respect and value others, so that pupils do the same and are encouraged to share their experiences and insights.*
>
> *Teachers, when they explicitly value others, shape pupils' and colleagues' perceptions of themselves. This helps them to recognise their unique talents, to feel special, and to have the confidence to succeed. It increases the motivation in all to achieve more than they ever thought they could.*
>
> *When teachers show that they respect others it becomes more likely that people throughout the school community will learn from others with diverse backgrounds, and learn to be good citizens.*

Anne takes great care in getting to know the pupils she teaches. In the interview, she told us that she visits each pupil in his or her home before they enter the school for the first time. Anne's class comprises individuals who come from a very diverse range of backgrounds. She values each one of these and the contribution each child can make to the group. In the interview, Anne talked about the unique nature of each individual and the special gifts they all possess.

The Key Elements identified earlier that exemplify the way in which Anne shows respect for others include:

- ▸ a warm approach that signals care

- ▸ energy, enthusiasm and patience – the eternal optimist!

C Planning and setting expectations – Information seeking

Under Professional Characteristics, and within the cluster of **C** Planning and setting expectations, the Hay McBer Report emphasizes the importance of *information seeking*. The report states that:

> *Effective teachers seek information about pupils, pupil attainment and progress, subject and curriculum content, best practice, and new developments in the school community and beyond.*

Effective Teachers in Primary Schools

Having a deeper understanding of pupils, their background, who they are, and their prior learning and attainment, helps teachers know what will interest and motivate them, so they can adapt their approach. As a result, pupils are likely to feel recognized and valued as individuals.

This capability is at the heart of accurate formative assessment. Teachers who continuously gather information about pupil progress and attainment are able to pace and adapt programmes of learning so they continue to be relevant and appropriate.

Finding appropriate resources and the best practice of others enhances teaching and learning, keeps approaches and programmes of work fresh, and avoids reinventing the wheel, ensuring effort is not wasted. Seeking out relevant inspection and research evidence can help improve planning and teaching.

Often the opportunity to gather information presents itself in the moment, so effective teachers are alert to connections and relevance, and have a drive to seize the information before the chance is lost.

Most importantly teachers who have a driving curiosity are modelling a characteristic that has always been key to learning, and is likely to be even more so in the future. This is a particularly contagious quality and rubs off on pupils – they become equally curious about their surroundings and why things are the way they are, and want to find out more for themselves.

As I've already said, Anne seeks out information about the class she teaches, including details about the children's backgrounds, with the view that this will inform her teaching. Anne speaks about how she has learned a great deal from other teachers and continues to do so. She continually, actively looks at new techniques of teaching and learning, including 'accelerated learning', to enhance her practice.

The Key Elements identified earlier that exemplify the way in which Anne demonstrates information seeking include:

▸ VAK input

▸ being a reflective practitioner.

E Relating to others – Understanding others

Under Professional Characteristics, and within the cluster of **E** Relating to others, the Hay McBer Report emphasizes the importance of *understanding others*. The report states that:

Effective teachers respond to pupils and others as individuals with unique gifts and talents. Having tuned in to pupils, teachers can sensitively frame approaches and tailor materials to take account of others' strengths, and the things that may have an adverse impact on learning. They may also identify enthusiasms or interests that can be used as a springboard for further learning.

People feel valued when they feel truly understood, and when other people take the trouble to find out who they are. Effective teachers are able to use this understanding, and go on to build pupils' self-esteem and gain their trust, knowing what is likely to motivate them as individuals.

Attending to others and their underlying feelings and concerns, so important in learning exchange, provides a model to pupils and others.

All individuals want to be understood. Children thrive in a classroom environment where they are made to feel wanted and special. Anne achieves this in the ways I have already described.

The Key Elements identified earlier that exemplify the way in which Anne demonstrates understanding others include:

> ‣ a warm approach that signals care

> ‣ energy, enthusiasm and patience – the eternal optimist!

> ‣ making learning fun

> ‣ being a reflective practitioner.

This table shows the teaching skill and professional characteristics identified in the analysis of Anne.

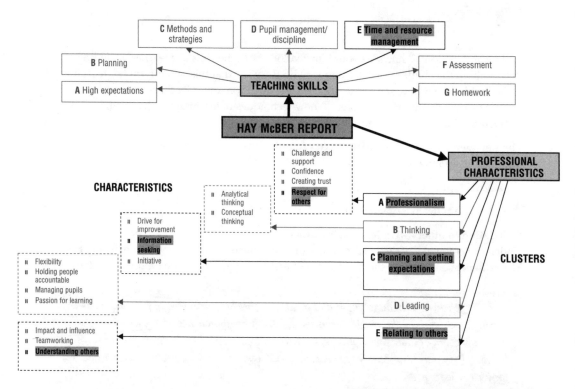

ANNE HENRY – Teaching Skills and Professional Characteristics identified in the analysis

Effective Teachers in Primary Schools

Mark Wilson

I see a context for ICT in every aspect of our curriculum.

Mark Wilson – VITAL Teacher Profile

Full Name:	Mark Wilson
Age when filmed:	34
School:	Primrose Hill Primary School (Leeds)
Number of pupils in the school:	350
Age range:	4–11
Age range Mark has taught:	Everything – reception through to 'A' level
Date Mark joined the school:	September 2001
Years of teaching in total:	7
Previous schools:	Westerton Primary School (Leeds)
	Advisory teacher for ICT (Leeds)
Year group taught in the DVD:	Year 6
Number of pupils in this class:	31

Mark Wilson – Key Elements

These are my initial ideas on some of the characteristics that combine to make Mark an effective teacher:

1 the use of modern technology in the classroom and keeping up to date with developments

2 setting out the learning objectives

3 adapting to potential problems during a lesson

4 mastery of the subject

5 working with the pupils

6 managing resources

7 high expectations

8 experience of a number of schools

9 reviewing learning objectives at the end of the lesson.

Key Element 1 – The use of modern technology in the classroom and keeping up to date with developments

This is the second of the lessons filmed for *Effective Teachers in Primary Schools* in which we can observe ICT being used in the classroom. (See also Alison Stoker.) ICT is spreading more and more throughout all lessons in all schools. We see here not only that Mark uses technology for presentation of the lesson but that the pupils also use computers in the lesson. Mark clearly has a commitment to ensuring that he keeps up to date with developments in ICT. The particular programs he used in the lesson filmed had only recently been released.

Key Element 2 – Setting out the learning objectives

Mark has the learning objectives written down on the board at the start of the lesson. The pupils can see, therefore, what the lesson is all about and where they are headed. Mark refers to the objectives again at the end of the lesson, ensuring that the class has a chance to reflect on what they have achieved and learned.

Key Element 3 – Adapting to potential problems during a lesson

All teachers know that even with the best plans things can go wrong in a lesson. In this lesson, the radio-mic used to pick up Mark's voice for the purposes of the filming in the classroom interferes with the laptops, which are radio controlled. The trick for a teacher is to remain calm. As you see on the video, Mark does not let this distract him from what he has to do, even though he obviously knows he is being filmed, and this creates added pressure. Eventually he has to allow the pupils to use the PCs to carry out their work.

Key Element 4 – Mastery of the subject

Mark is in the fortunate position of having been an ICT advisory teacher. He therefore feels very comfortable with the use of ICT in the classroom. However mastery of the subject is achieved, it is important for a teacher to be knowledgeable about the subjects he or she teaches.

Key Element 5 – Working with the pupils

All effective teachers display the ability to get close to children and work with them so that learning becomes almost a joint exercise. Mark works closely with the pupils, making each one feel special and important. There is a balanced input of individual and whole-class teaching. (See 'Are certain teaching styles more effective?' in Section Two.)

Key Element 6 – Managing resources

In the interview, Mark explains that he feels it is absolutely essential for the resources required to be readily available during a lesson. He ensures that all the materials the pupils require are on the tables before the lesson starts. Organization and planning are crucial to the success of any lesson.

Key Element 7 – High expectations

Pupils tend to be what they are told they are. They also tend to be what the teacher expects them to be. Mark demands a high level of understanding from his class. His high expectations are rewarded by a high calibre of work from the pupils.

Key Element 8 – Experience of a number of schools

Mark has worked in several schools as an adviser. He has therefore experienced a number of different teaching styles and methods. Still, he feels he is learning. Clearly, not every teacher will have the opportunity to experience as many schools as Mark but we can all learn by looking at each other's teaching and I believe this is what happens in good schools, where peer observations become the norm.

Key Element 9 – Reviewing learning objectives at the end of the lesson

As a conclusion, revisiting the learning objectives given at the start of the lesson is a useful way of reinforcing the message that a number of things have been learned. It is also a way of helping pupils to absorb the newly acquired knowledge and understanding more effectively.

Mark Wilson – direct links with the Hay McBer Report

The following describes the links I have made between Mark's teaching and the Hay McBer Report. As for all the teachers, I have chosen one Teaching Skill and three Professional Characteristics.

Teaching Skill

The Teaching Skill from the Hay McBer Report that I have chosen to link Mark with is:

   B Planning.

Two of four key questions the Hay McBer Report asks about 'planning' are:

> ▸ *Does the teacher communicate a clear plan and objectives for the lesson at the start of the lesson?*
>
> ▸ *Does the teacher review what pupils have learned at the end of the lesson?*

We see on the video Mark doing both of these things. It helps pupils to understand the structure of the lesson – allowing them to have an insight into the 'big picture'. The Hay McBer Report adds:

> *Effective teachers are good at planning, setting a clear framework and objectives for each lesson. The effective teacher is very systematic in the preparation for, and execution of, each lesson. The lesson planning is done in the context of the broader curriculum and longer-term plans.*

In addition, the report says:

> *For pupils, there is clarity of what they are doing, where they are going and how they will know when they have achieved the objectives of the lesson. Effective teachers create the time to review lesson objectives and learning outcomes at the end of each lesson.*

Mark makes it clear through a review at the end of the lesson exactly what the children have learned.

Professional Characteristics

The three Professional Characteristics from the Hay McBer Report that I have chosen to link Mark with are shown below.

Cluster	Characteristics
A Professionalism	II Challenge and support
B Thinking	II Analytical thinking
C Planning and setting expectations	II Drive for improvement

A Professionalism – Challenge and support
Under Professional Characteristics, and within the cluster of **A** Professionalism, the Hay McBer Report emphasizes the importance of *challenge and support*. The report states that:

> *Caring about the whole child and its learning, and communicating this through action, is an essential part of building the self-esteem needed for learning to take place.*
>
> *Expressing positive expectations of pupils – that they can and will learn and be successful – is one of the most powerful ways to influence pupils and raise achievement. It is one of the*

> distinctive behaviours of high performing teachers who radiate confidence in their pupils and their potential, and never give up on them.
>
> Pupils only get one chance to have their school education. They are entitled to expect the best possible provision. Effective teachers therefore not only care, but also take a firm line. This means they refuse to accept mediocrity or second best provision, and challenge others – parents, colleagues and pupils themselves – in the best interests of the pupil.
>
> This tough caring is particularly important in meeting the requirements of pupils with special needs, including those of high ability. It is an important part of a drive to address the needs of all pupils.

Mark sets a high level of challenge for the group he teaches. He expresses a sense of trust in them being able to manage the task. His confidence is rewarded by the pupils also having high expectations of themselves.

The Key Elements identified earlier that exemplify the way in which Mark demonstrates challenge and support include:

- ▸ mastery of the subject
- ▸ high expectations.

B Thinking – Analytical thinking

Under Professional Characteristics, and within the cluster of **B** Thinking, the Hay McBer Report emphasizes the importance of *analytical thinking*. The report states that:

> Planning programmes of work requires a focus on evidence and data relating to pupils and their attainments. Data can be quantitative: for example, about prior attainment, progression data, inspection findings; or qualitative, such as views and opinions.
>
> Thoroughness in preparation, based on an accurate assessment of the stage pupils have reached – for the lesson, the term and the year – creates a framework for teaching and learning. Objectives and learning outcomes need to be clearly set out. Learning should be split into easily digested parts that make sense and have a logical flow. Milestones need to be specified so that pupils have a sense of progress and can measure their achievements against learning objectives.
>
> By demonstrating analytical thinking themselves, and asking why, teachers can show pupils the importance of a logical approach and get them to question why they are doing what they do on a regular basis.
>
> Analytical thinking also helps to monitor pupils' progress, so that teaching schemes can be regularly adjusted to accommodate learning differences and other variables. Reflecting on degrees of success, and analysing why some things went better than others, is crucial. It helps not only by encouraging a flexible approach, lesson by lesson, but also in making improvements year on year, and improving professional practice.

Mark demonstrates a thoroughness of planning in his lesson in which he has analysed the requirements of his class and considered the most appropriate methods to use to fully engage them in the work. Part of his analysis is to ensure that the class is able to experience new

---

ICT packages that offer an alternative method of learning concepts and factual information. Through his experience as an advisory teacher, he has had the opportunity of analysing a number of different approaches to teaching, which he can use with the pupils he teaches.

The Key Elements identified earlier that exemplify the way in which Mark shows analytical thinking include:

- the use of modern technology in the classroom and keeping up to date with developments
- experience of a number of schools.

C Planning and setting expectations – Drive for improvement
Under Professional Characteristics, and within the cluster of **C** Planning and setting expectations, the Hay McBer Report emphasizes the importance of *drive for improvement*. The report states that:

> *Setting stretching and achievable targets, taking past performance into account, makes attainment more likely. Measuring and affirming improvement motivates pupils and others. This creates a focus on excellence and lays down exactly what is to be achieved. Measuring progress and results provides motivation for pupils and others. This is about moving out of the comfort zone and providing challenge and excitement in the learning process.*
>
> *Achieving more than you ever thought possible builds self-esteem. Success breeds success. The more pupils achieve, the more they believe they will succeed. This makes them want to achieve more, leading to more success, not only as classroom learners but in life.*
>
> *The commitment of teachers to their own continuing professional development reminds them of what it is like to be a learner, and helps them develop their own skills and characteristics. This helps them to empathize with pupils, and models the importance of continuous lifelong learning. In this way the school becomes a genuine learning community with a vibrancy and liveliness about it – making pupils want to be there and to participate.*

A number of the Professional Characteristics in the Hay McBer Report are inextricably linked. There is a clear link here between *Drive for improvement* and *Challenge and support*, with which Mark was linked earlier. To add to the previous comments, it is true to say that Mark is committed to his own professional development. This is evidenced by his earlier interest in being an advisory teacher and his move now back into schools. Mark wants to keep up with developments in teaching, particularly with ICT. This will influence the way that the pupils themselves view their own learning and serves as a good role model for lifelong learning. Mark takes the pupils out of their personal 'comfort zone' to challenge and extend them.

The Key Elements identified earlier that exemplify the way in which Mark shows a drive for improvement include:

- managing resources
- high expectations
- experience of a number of schools.

This table shows the teaching skill and professional characteristics identified in the analysis of Mark.

Effective Teachers in Primary Schools

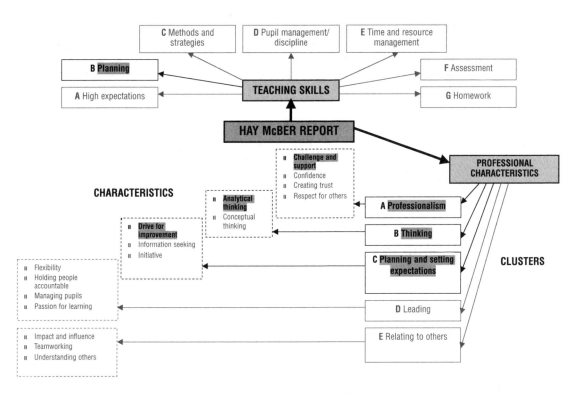

CHARACTERISTICS

CLUSTERS

MARK WILSON – Teaching Skills and Professional Characteristics identified in the analysis

Sarah Lancaster

 I definitely think I'm getting better, the more experience I have. You just pick up different things from different schools and watching different teachers work – listening to the way they interact with the children. You can learn to adapt it to your own way of teaching. I always think that you can learn something from every lesson.

Sarah Lancaster – VITAL Teacher Profile

Full Name:	Sarah Lancaster
Age when filmed:	33
School:	Parish Church School (Skipton, North Yorkshire)
Number of pupils in the school:	365
Age range:	4–11
Age range Sarah has taught:	5–11
Date Sarah joined the school:	September 2001
Years of teaching in total:	7
Previous schools:	Cowling C P School (West Yorkshire)
	Carleton C of E Primary (Skipton, North Yorkshire)
Year group taught in the DVD:	Year 1
Number of pupils in this class:	24

Sarah Lancaster – Key Elements

These are my initial ideas on some of the characteristics that combine to make Sarah an effective teacher:

1 classroom environment

2 resources

3 encouraging participation with positive comments

4 VAK input

5 classroom presence

6 clear and precise instructions

7 being close to the pupils

8 varied work

9 pupils make contributions.

Key Element 1 – Classroom environment

Bright and colourful displays are a feature common to so many primary school classrooms. The care taken by teachers in this respect shows how they are prepared to go beyond the essentials of what is required of them to provide a rich environment in which pupils can feel comfortable and at home.

Key Element 2 – Resources

Sarah demonstrates here some of the resources developed as a consequence of the National Curriculum. All pupils are given the opportunity to respond to questions, for example, by holding up their individual answers on specially produced cards.

Key Element 3 – Encouraging participation with positive comments

It becomes quite a natural part of the act of many teachers that they constantly give pupils confidence through the use of positive feedback. Here, Sarah uses comments such as 'Thinking carefully – good boy', and 'Well done, Georgina'.

Key Element 4 – VAK input

Sarah provides a number of Visual, Auditory and Kinesthetic inputs to the lesson. Like many teachers in recent years, Sarah is aware of the need to provide inputs that match the dominant ways in which different pupils access information.

Key Element 5 – Classroom presence

People sometimes argue that a teacher either has 'classroom presence' or has not. There is little doubt that some teachers are blessed or gifted in this respect but there are learned strategies that can be used to enhance the classroom presence of any teacher. These include being aware of and working on the use of the voice, body language and the position adopted in the classroom. Sarah speaks to the class in a precise and calm fashion and adopts different positions in the classroom to send out different messages to the class.

Key Element 6 – Clear and precise instructions

In some respects, this follows on from the last Key Element. Sarah makes the purpose of the lesson very clear to the class through guidance that leaves no uncertainty about the aims and objectives of the lesson.

Key Element 7 – Being close to the pupils

Sarah demonstrates how effective teachers will work closely with pupils to explain concepts and bring about a sense of shared working.

Key Element 8 – Varied work

Sarah uses a range of whole-class teaching, group and individual work. Different pupils will discover that they work best in certain ways. A variety of listening and watching the teacher demonstrate certain things, working individually with the teacher, working in groups and working individually alone will enable pupils to experience working in one or more of their preferred ways.

Key Element 9 – Pupils make contributions

Sarah invites pupils to come out to the front of the classroom to contribute their suggestions, encourages the use of the number cards to provide answers and elicits individual responses as she goes around the classroom. In this way, she ensures that pupils are given the opportunity to contribute to the lesson in a variety of ways.

Sarah Lancaster – direct links with the Hay McBer Report

The following describes the links I have made between Sarah's teaching and the Hay McBer Report. As for all the teachers, I have chosen one Teaching Skill and three Professional Characteristics.

Teaching Skill

The Teaching Skill from the Hay McBer Report that I have chosen to link Sarah with is:

　A High expectations.

Two of five key questions the Hay McBer Report asks about 'high expectations' are:

> ▸ *Does the teacher vary motivational strategies for different individuals?*
>
> ▸ *Does the teacher provide opportunities for students to take responsibility for their own learning?*

Sarah uses a range of strategies, from whole-class teaching to individual and group work.

> *Effective teachers set high expectations for the pupils and communicate them directly to the pupils. They challenge and inspire pupils, expecting the most from them, so as to deepen their knowledge and understanding.*

An effective teacher can set high expectations implicitly through the tasks they present to the pupils. The work on number-lines observed here, for example, is complex but Sarah encourages the pupils through her belief that they will be able to do the work.

In addition, the Hay McBer Report says:

> *Effective teachers are relentless in their pursuit of a standard of excellence to be achieved by all pupils, and in holding fast to this ambition. These expectations are high, clear and consistent.*

Professional Characteristics

The three Professional Characteristics from the Hay McBer Report that I have chosen to link Sarah with are shown below.

Cluster	Characteristics
B Thinking **C** Planning and setting expectations **D** Leading	ll Conceptual thinking ll Initiative ll Managing pupils

B Thinking – Conceptual thinking

Under Professional Characteristics, and within the cluster of **B** Thinking, the Hay McBer Report emphasizes the importance of *conceptual thinking*. The report states that:

> *Effective teachers develop lessons and programmes of work which deliver the curriculum in such a way that they provide breadth, balance and continuity, and match the level and needs of their classes and the individuals within them. They therefore move easily between the big picture and the detail.*
>
> *They also make links between areas of the curriculum, so that learning can be consolidated across different subjects, and think about connections they see outside the classroom and beyond the school, to enhance and enrich teaching and learning.*
>
> *Pupils will progress if they fully understand concepts and subject content, so the ability to clarify and simplify complex ideas and communicate them is very important.*

Sarah uses her voice to great effect to communicate her ideas to the class. She also uses the visual aid of a flip chart and the pupils are involved in thinking and presenting their answers (kinesthetic) to the class as a whole. She goes around the room working with individuals to ensure concepts are fully understood. Sarah helps pupils and others to understand something complex by finding a new and creative way to explain it in simple terms.

The Key Elements identified earlier that exemplify the way in which Sarah shows conceptual thinking include:

- clear and precise instructions
- being close to the pupils
- varied work.

C Planning and setting expectations – Initiative

Under Professional Characteristics, and within the cluster of C Planning and setting expectations, the Hay McBer Report emphasizes the importance of *initiative*. The report states that:

> In addition to the careful planning of mainstream lessons and programmes of work, effective teachers think ahead. This enriches the curriculum and makes learning relevant and coherent, and enables planning of special events, or being able to tie in programmes of work with local, national or world events.
>
> Technology is reshaping future teaching and learning methods, and effective teachers think ahead to take advantage of opportunities this and other developments provide. They are ahead of the game, so they can make lessons and programmes of work relevant to the way life will be for pupils after they leave school.
>
> The ability to act immediately and decisively is important – to give and take in a hectic, fast-moving school environment with pupils who are lively and energetic; to deal with problems before they escalate; and to seize opportunities. Alert, action-oriented teachers stand out, and command respect, with colleagues as well as pupils.

Sarah is very active and energetic in the classroom. All classrooms are busy, hectic places where it is vitally important that the teacher should both appear to be, and actually be, in control at all times. Sarah manages the various demands placed upon her with calm sensitivity. Pupils in Sarah's class will be aware of the 'lighthouse effect' she operates. This is what the Hay McBer Report refers to as the habitual scanning by which effective teachers appear to pick up everything that is going on.

The Key Elements identified earlier that exemplify the way in which Sarah shows initiative include:

- classroom environment
- VAK input
- classroom presence.

D Leading – Managing pupils

Under Professional Characteristics, and within the cluster of D Leading, the Hay McBer Report emphasizes the importance of *managing pupils*. The report states that:

This characteristic is key among all the characteristics in the model in creating a climate in the classroom, and in the wider school community, that drives improved outcomes in terms of pupil attainment and their spiritual, moral and cultural development. This is because managing pupils well creates clarity about direction, and emphasizes standards and performance improvement, two key drivers for raising achievement.

This direct, causal link with performance is a measure of the teacher's success in motivating pupils. It matters because it generates and focuses the extra effort everyone can bring.

The issue of managing pupils is obviously a vast topic. A teacher who manages pupils well gets the very best from them and encourages them to contribute to the growth and development of the group as well. Sarah speaks positively to the class, building up their self-esteem, and ensures that all pupils are involved in the task. She creates a positive, upbeat atmosphere, which includes an environment where pupils can succeed.

The Key Elements identified earlier that exemplify the way in which Sarah demonstrates her skill in managing pupils include:

▸ pupils make contributions

▸ being close to the pupils

▸ clear and precise instructions.

This table shows the teaching skill and professional characteristics identified in the analysis of Sarah.

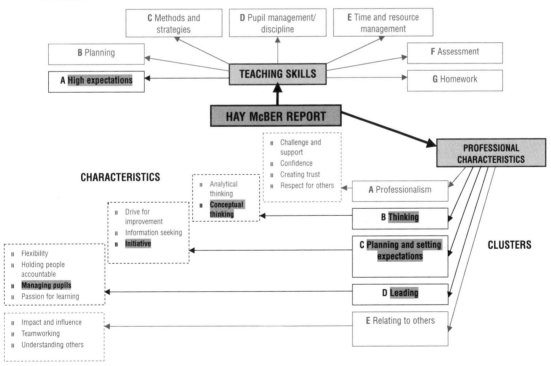

SARAH LANCASTER – Teaching Skills and Professional Characteristics identified in the analysis

Appendix 1: Linking Hay McBer Analysis with the Professional Standards for Teachers

Teaching Skills Observation Form

Note: References below refer to the Core Standards. For example C1 refers to Core Standard C1 in the Professional Standards for Teachers.

Date:	Teacher:
Lesson:	Observer:

Heading	Observations
1 High expectations Links with Core Standards C1 and C2	
2 Planning Links with Core Standards C3, C26 and C29	
3 Methods and strategies Links with Core Standards C29	
4 Pupil management/discipline Links with Core Standards C38 and C39	
5 Time and resource management	
6 Assessment Links with Core Standards C11, C12 and C13	
7 Homework Links with Core Standards C28 and C31	

Hay McBer – Professional Characteristics Observation Form

Date:	Teacher:
Lesson:	Observer:

Cluster	Tick characteristics to be observed	Observations
1 Professionalism	Challenge and support Confidence Creating trust Respect for others	
2 Thinking	Analytical thinking Conceptual thinking	
3 Planning and setting expectations	Drive for improvement Information seeking Initiative	
4 Leading	Flexibility Holding people accountable Managing pupils Passion for learning	
5 Relating to others	Impact and influence Teamworking Understanding others	

Hay McBer – Classroom Climate Observation Form

Date:	Teacher:
Lesson:	Observer:

Climate dimension	Observations
1 Clarity	
2 Order	
3 Standards	
4 Fairness	
5 Participation	
6 Support	
7 Safety	
8 Interest	
9 Environment	

Appendix 2: Hay McBer Observation Guidance Criteria

Teaching Skills Guidance

Heading	Key Questions as Guidance
1 High expectations Links with Core Standards C1 and C2	1 Does the teacher encourage high standards of: • Effort? • Accuracy? • Presentation? 2 Does the teacher use differentiation appropriately to challenge all pupils in the class? 3 Does the teacher vary motivational strategies for different individuals? 4 Does the teacher provide opportunities for students to take responsibility for their own learning? 5 Does the teacher draw on pupil experiences or ideas relevant to the lesson?
2 Planning Links with Core Standards C3, C26 and C29	1 Does the teacher communicate a clear plan and objectives for the lesson at the start of the lesson? 2 Does the teacher have the necessary materials and resources ready for the class? 3 Does the teacher link lesson objectives to the national curriculum? 4 Does the teacher review what pupils have learned at the end of the lesson?
3 Methods and strategies Links with Core Standard C29	1 Does the teacher involve all pupils in the lesson? 2 Does the teacher use a variety of activities/learning methods? 3 Does the teacher apply teaching methods appropriate to the National Curriculum? 4 Does the teacher use a variety of questioning techniques to probe pupils' knowledge and understanding? 5 Does the teacher encourage pupils to use a variety of problem-solving techniques? 6 Does the teacher give clear instructions and explanations? 7 Does practical activity have a clear purpose in improving pupils' understanding or achievement? 8 Does the teacher listen and respond to pupils?
4 Pupil management/discipline Links with Core Standards C38 and C39	1 Does the teacher keep pupils on task throughout the lesson? 2 Does the teacher correct bad behaviour immediately? 3 Does the teacher praise good achievement and effort? 4 Does the teacher treat different children fairly? 5 Does the teacher manage non-pupils (support teachers/staff) well?
5 Time and resource management	1 Does the teacher structure the lesson to use the time available well? 2 Does the lesson last for the planned time? 3 Are the appropriate learning resources used to enhance pupils' opportunities? 4 Does the teacher use an appropriate pace? 5 Does the teacher allocate his/her time fairly amongst pupils?
6 Assessment Links with Core Standards C11, C12 and C13	1 Does the teacher focus on understanding and meaning, factual memory, skills mastery and application in real-life settings? 2 Does the teacher use tests, competitions, etc. to assess understanding? 3 Does the teacher recognize misconceptions and clear them up? 4 Is there evidence of pupils' written work having been marked or otherwise assessed? 5 Does the teacher encourage pupils to do better next time?
7 Homework Links with Core Standards C28 and C31	1 Is the homework set either to consolidate or extend the coverage of the lesson? 2 Is homework which had been set previously followed up in the lesson? 3 Does the teacher explain what learning objectives pupils will gain from homework?

Hay McBer Observation Guidance Criteria

Professional Characteristics Guidance

Cluster	Tick Characteristics to be Observed	Guidance
1 Professionalism	• Challenge and support	A commitment to do everything possible for each pupil and enable all pupils to be successful.
	• Confidence	The belief in one's ability to be effective and to take on challenges.
	• Creating trust	Being consistent and fair. Keeping one's word.
	• Respect for others	The underlying belief that individuals matter and deserve respect.
2 Thinking	• Analytical thinking	The ability to think logically, break things down, and recognize cause and effect.
	• Conceptual thinking	The ability to see patterns and links, even when there is a lot of detail.
3 Planning and setting expectations	• Drive for improvement	Relentless energy for setting and meeting challenging targets, for pupils and the school.
	• Information seeking	A drive to find out more and get to the heart of things; intellectual curiosity.
	• Initiative	The drive to act now to anticipate and pre-empt events.
4 Leading	• Flexibility	The ability and willingness to adapt to the needs of a situation and change tactics.
	• Holding people accountable	The drive and ability to set clear expectations and parameters and to hold others accountable for performance.
	• Managing pupils	The drive and the ability to provide clear direction to pupils, and to enthuse and motivate them.
	• Passion for learning	The drive and ability to support pupils in their learning, and how to help them become confident and independent learners.
5 Relating to others	• Impact and influence	The ability and the drive to produce positive outcomes by impressing and influencing others.
	• Teamworking	The ability to work with others to achieve shared goals.
	• Understanding others	The drive and ability to understand others, and why they behave as they do.

Hay McBer Observation Guidance Criteria

Classroom Climate Guidance

Climate dimension	Guidance
1 Clarity	Clarity around the purpose of each lesson. How each lesson relates to the broader subject, as well as clarity regarding the aims and objectives of the school.
2 Order	Order within the classroom, where discipline, order and civilized behaviour are maintained.
3 Standards	A clear set of standards as to how pupils should behave and what each pupil should do and try to achieve, with a clear focus on higher rather than minimum standards.
4 Fairness	Fairness: the degree to which there is an absence of favouritism, and a consistent link between rewards in the classroom and actual performance.
5 Participation	Participation: the opportunity for pupils to participate actively in the class by discussion, questioning, giving out materials, and other similar activities.
6 Support	Support: feeling emotionally supported in the classroom, so that pupils are willing to try new things and learn from mistakes.
7 Safety	Safety: the degree to which the classroom is a safe place, where pupils are not at risk from emotional bullying, or other fear-rousing factors.
8 Interest	Interest: the feeling that the classroom is an interesting and exciting place to be, where pupils feel stimulated to learn.
9 Environment	Environment: the feeling that the classroom is a comfortable, well-organized, clean and attractive physical environment.

Appendix 3: Hay McBer Teaching Skills Forms – *for Self-analysis or Observation*

1. High expectations

Links with Core Standards C1 and C2

Effective teachers communicate high, clear and consistent expectations with an appropriate level of challenge to all pupils.

Key questions	Examples of how I do this
Does the teacher encourage high standards of effort, accuracy and presentation?	
Does the teacher use differentiation appropriately to challenge all pupils in the class?	
Does the teacher vary motivational strategies for different individuals?	
Does the teacher provide opportunities for students to take responsibility for their own learning?	
Does the teacher draw on pupil experiences or ideas relevant to the lesson?	

For free downloads of all these forms go to www.ecmconnections.co.uk

2. Planning

Links with Core Standards C3, C26 and C29

Effective teachers have a clear plan and objectives for each lesson. They communicate these clearly to pupils at the start of the session. They focus on pupils' learning outcomes. Learning activities have clear instructions.

Key questions	Examples of how I do this
Does the teacher communicate a clear plan and objectives for the lesson at the start of the lesson?	
Does the teacher have the necessary materials and resources ready for the class?	
Does the teacher link lesson objectives to the National Curriculum?	
Does the teacher review what pupils have learned at the end of the lesson?	

For free downloads of all these forms go to www.ecmconnections.co.uk

---

3. Methods and strategies

Links with Core Standard C29

Effective teachers use a variety of teaching strategies and techniques. They teach actively, interact a lot with pupils, and monitor their understanding. They keep pupils engaged and on task in class, small group and individual activities.

Key questions	Examples of how I do this
Does the teacher involve all pupils in the lesson?	
Does the teacher use a variety of activities/learning methods?	
Does the teacher apply teaching methods appropriate to the National Curriculum objectives?	
Does the teacher use a variety of questioning techniques to probe pupils' knowledge and understanding?	
Does the teacher encourage pupils to use a variety of problem-solving techniques?	
Does the teacher give clear instructions and explanations?	
Does practical activity have a clear purpose in improving pupils' understanding or achievement?	
Does the teacher listen and respond to pupils?	

For free downloads of all these forms go to www.ecmconnections.co.uk

Effective Teachers in Primary Schools

4. Pupil management/discipline

Links with Core Standards C38 and C39

Effective teachers have a clear strategy for pupil management and communicate clear and effective boundaries for pupils' behaviour. Pupils feel safe and secure, and maximum time is focused on learning.

Key questions	Examples of how I do this
Does the teacher keep the pupils on task throughout the lesson?	
Does the teacher correct bad behaviour immediately?	
Does the teacher praise good achievement and effort?	
Does the teacher treat different children fairly?	
Does the teacher manage non-pupils (support teachers/ staff) well?	

For free downloads of all these forms go to www.ecmconnections.co.uk

5. Time and resource management

Effective teachers make full use of planned time, start promptly, maintain a brisk pace and finish with a succinct review of learning. They allocate their time fairly amongst pupils.

Key questions	Examples of how I do this
Does the teacher structure the lesson to use the time available well?	
Does the lesson last for the planned time?	
Are appropriate learning resources used to enhance pupils' opportunities?	
Does the teacher use an appropriate pace?	
Does the teacher allocate his/her time fairly amongst pupils?	

For free downloads of all these forms go to www.ecmconnections.co.uk

Effective Teachers in Primary Schools

6. Assessment

Links with Core Standards C11, C12 and C13

Effective teachers make use of a range of assessment methods to monitor pupils' progress, their gaps in knowledge and areas of misunderstanding. They give feedback and encourage pupils to judge their own success and set themselves targets.

Key questions	Examples of how I do this
Does the teacher focus on understanding and meaning, factual memory, skills mastery and applications in real-life settings?	
Does the teacher use tests, competitions, etc. to assess understanding?	
Does the teacher recognize misconceptions and clear them up?	
Is there evidence of pupils' written work having been marked or otherwise assessed?	
Does the teacher encourage pupils to do better next time?	

For free downloads of all these forms go to www.ecmconnections.co.uk

7. Homework

Links with Core Standards C28 and C31

The regular setting of homework, in primary and secondary schools, is an important part of the assessment process. Effective teachers ensure that homework is integrated with class work, is tailored to individual needs and is marked regularly and constructively.

Key questions	Examples of how I do this
Is homework set either to consolidate or extend the coverage of the lesson?	
Is homework, which had been set previously, followed up in the lesson?	
Does the teacher explain what learning objectives pupils will gain from homework?	

For free downloads of all these forms go to www.ecmconnections.co.uk

Effective Teachers in Primary Schools

Appendix 4: Hay McBer Professional Characteristics Forms – *for Self-analysis or Observation*

1. Professionalism

Characteristic	Self-analysis or Observation
Challenge and support A commitment to do everything possible for each pupil and enable all pupils to be successful.	
Confidence The belief in one's ability to be effective and to take on challenges.	
Creating trust Being consistent and fair. Keeping one's word.	
Respect for others The underlying belief that individuals matter and deserve respect.	

For free downloads of all these forms go to www.ecmconnections.co.uk

2. Thinking

Characteristic	Self-analysis or Observation
Analytical thinking The ability to think logically, break things down and recognize cause and effect.	
Conceptual thinking The ability to see patterns and links, even when there is a lot of detail.	

For free downloads of all these forms go to www.ecmconnections.co.uk

Effective Teachers in Primary Schools

3. Planning and setting expectations

Characteristic	Self-analysis or Observation
Drive for improvement Relentless energy for setting and meeting challenging targets, for pupils and the school.	
Information seeking A drive to find out more and get to the heart of things; intellectual curiosity.	
Initiative The drive to act now to anticipate and pre-empt events.	

For free downloads of all these forms go to www.ecmconnections.co.uk

4. Leading

Characteristic	Self-analysis or Observation
Flexibility The ability and willingness to adapt to the needs of a situation and change tactics.	
Holding people accountable The drive and ability to set clear expectations and parameters and to hold others accountable for performance.	
Managing pupils The drive and the ability to provide clear direction to pupils, and to enthuse and motivate them.	
Passion for learning The drive and ability to support pupils in their learning, and how to help them become confident and independent learners.	

For free downloads of all these forms go to www.ecmconnections.co.uk

Effective Teachers in Primary Schools

5. Relating to others

Characteristic	Self-analysis or Observation
Impact and influence The ability and the drive to produce positive outcomes by impressing and influencing others.	
Teamworking The ability to work with others to achieve shared goals.	
Understanding others The drive and ability to understand others, and why they behave as they do.	

For free downloads of all these forms go to www.ecmconnections.co.uk

Appendix 5: Hay McBer – Classroom Climate Forms – *for Self-analysis or Observation*

Key dimension	Self-analysis or Observation
1. Clarity Clarity around the purpose of each lesson. How each lesson relates to the broader subject, as well as clarity regarding the aims and objectives of the school.	
2. Order Order within the classroom, where discipline, order and civilized behaviour are maintained.	
3. Standards A clear set of standards as to how pupils should behave and what each pupil should do and try to achieve, with a clear focus on higher rather than minimum standards.	

For free downloads of all these forms go to www.ecmconnections.co.uk

Key dimension	Self-analysis or Observation
4. Fairness The degree to which there is an absence of favouritism, and a consistent link between rewards in the classroom and actual performance.	
5. Participation The opportunity for pupils to participate actively in the class by discussion, questioning, giving out materials, and other similar activities.	
6. Support Feeling emotionally supported in the classroom, so that pupils are willing to try new things and learn from mistakes.	

For free downloads of all these forms go to www.ecmconnections.co.uk

Key dimension	Self-analysis or Observation
7. Safety The degree to which the classroom is a safe place, where pupils are not at risk from emotional bullying, or other fear-rousing factors.	
8. Interest The feeling that the classroom is an interesting and exciting place to be, where pupils feel stimulated to learn.	
9. Environment The feeling that the classroom is a comfortable, well-organized, clean and attractive physical environment.	

For free downloads of all these forms go to www.ecmconnections.co.uk

Effective Teachers in Primary Schools

Appendix 6: Professional Standards for Teachers – QTS Criteria

1. Professional attributes

Relationships with children and young people	
Q1	Have high expectations of children and young people including a commitment to ensuring that they can achieve their full educational potential and to establishing fair, respectful, trusting, supportive and constructive relationships with them.
Q2	Demonstrate the positive values, attitudes and behaviour they expect from children and young people.
Frameworks	
Q3	(a) Be aware of the professional duties of teachers and the statutory framework within which they work. (b) Be aware of the policies and practices of the workplace and share in collective responsibility for their implementation.
Communicating and working with others	
Q4	Communicate effectively with children, young people, colleagues, parents and carers.
Q5	Recognize and respect the contribution that colleagues, parents and carers can make to the development and well-being of children and young people, and to raising their levels of attainment.
Q6	Have a commitment to collaboration and co-operative working
Personal professional development	
Q7	(a) Reflect on and improve their practice, and take responsibility for identifying and meeting their developing professional needs. (b) Identify priorities for their early professional development in the context of induction.
Q8	Have a creative and constructively critical approach towards innovation, being prepared to adapt their practice where benefits and improvements are identified.
Q9	Act upon advice and feedback and be open to coaching and mentoring.

For free downloads of all these forms go to www.ecmconnections.co.uk

2. Professional knowledge and understanding

Teaching and learning	
Q10	Have a knowledge and understanding of a range of teaching, learning and behaviour management strategies and know how to use and adapt them, including how to personalize learning and provide opportunities for all learners to achieve their potential.
Assessment and monitoring	
Q11	Know the assessment requirements and arrangements for the subjects/curriculum areas they are trained to teach, including those relating to public examinations and qualifications.
Q12	Know a range of approaches to assessment, including the importance of formative assessment.
Q13	Know how to use local and national statistical information to evaluate the effectiveness of their teaching, to monitor the progress of those they teach and to raise levels of attainment.
Subjects and curriculum	
Q14	Have a secure knowledge and understanding of their subjects/curriculum areas and related pedagogy to enable them to teach effectively across the age and ability range for which they are trained.
Q15	Know and understand the relevant statutory and non-statutory curricula and frameworks, including those provided through the National Strategies, for their subjects/curriculum areas, and other relevant initiatives applicable to the age and ability range for which they are trained.
Literacy, numeracy and ICT	
Q16	Have passed the professional skills tests in numeracy, literacy and information and communications technology (ICT).
Q17	Know how to use skills in literacy, numeracy and ICT to support their teaching and wider professional activities.
Achievement and diversity	
Q18	Understand how children and young people develop and how the progress, rate of development and well-being of learners are affected by a range of developmental, social, religious, ethnic, cultural and linguistic influences.
Q19	Know how to make effective personalized provision for those they teach, including those for whom English is an additional language or who have special educational needs or disabilities, and how to take practical account of diversity and promote equality and inclusion in their teaching.
Q20	Know and understand the roles of colleagues with specific responsibilities, including those with responsibility for learners with special educational needs and disabilities and other individual learning needs.
Health and well-being	
Q21	(a) Be aware of the current legal requirements, national policies and guidance on the safeguarding and promotion of the well-being of children and young people. (b) Know how to identify and support children and young people whose progress, development or well-being is affected by changes or difficulties in their personal circumstances, and when to refer them to colleagues for specialist support.

For free downloads of all these forms go to www.ecmconnections.co.uk

3. Professional skills

Planning	
Q22	Plan for progression across the age and ability range for which they are trained, designing effective learning sequences within lessons and across series of lessons and demonstrating secure subject/curriculum knowledge.
Q23	Design opportunities for learners to develop their literacy, numeracy and ICT skills.
Q24	Plan homework or other out-of-class work to sustain learners' progress and to extend and consolidate their learning.

Teaching	
Q25	Teach lessons and sequences of lessons across the age and ability range for which they are trained in which they: (a) use a range of teaching strategies and resources, including e-learning, taking practical account of diversity and promoting equality and inclusion (b) build on prior knowledge, develop concepts and processes, enable learners to apply new knowledge, understanding and skills and meet learning objectives (c) adapt their language to suit the learners they teach, introducing new ideas and concepts clearly, and using explanations, questions, discussions and plenaries effectively (d) demonstrate the ability to manage the learning of individuals, groups and whole classes, modifying their teaching to suit the stage of the lesson.

Assessing, monitoring and giving feedback	
Q26	(a) Make effective use of a range of assessment, monitoring and recording strategies. (b) Assess the learning needs of those they teach in order to set challenging learning objectives.
Q27	Provide timely, accurate and constructive feedback on learners' attainment, progress and areas for development.
Q28	Support and guide learners to reflect on their learning, identify the progress they have made and identify their emerging learning needs.

Reviewing teaching and learning	
Q29	Evaluate the impact of their teaching on the progress of all learners, and modify their planning and classroom practice where necessary.

Learning environment	
Q30	Establish a purposeful and safe learning environment conducive to learning and identify opportunities for learners to learn in out-of-school contexts.
Q31	Establish a clear framework for classroom discipline to manage learners' behaviour constructively and promote their self-control and independence.

Teamworking and collaboration	
Q32	Work as a team member and identify opportunities for working with colleagues, sharing the development of effective practice with them.
Q33	Ensure that colleagues working with them are appropriately involved in supporting learning and understand the roles they are expected to fulfil.

For free downloads of all these forms go to www.ecmconnections.co.uk

Appendix 7: Professional Standards for Teachers – QTS Forms

1. Professional attributes

Relationships with children and young people		Evidence
Q1	Have high expectations of children and young people including a commitment to ensuring that they can achieve their full educational potential and to establishing fair, respectful, trusting, supportive and constructive relationships with them.	
Q2	Demonstrate the positive values, attitudes and behaviour they expect from children and young people.	
Frameworks		**Evidence**
Q3	(a) Be aware of the professional duties of teachers and the statutory framework within which they work. (b) Be aware of the policies and practices of the workplace and share in collective responsibility for their implementation.	
Communicating and working with others		**Evidence**
Q4	Communicate effectively with children, young people, colleagues, parents and carers.	
Q5	Recognize and respect the contribution that colleagues, parents and carers can make to the development and well-being of children and young people, and to raising their levels of attainment.	
Q6	Have a commitment to collaboration and cooperative working.	
Personal professional development		**Evidence**
Q7	(a) Reflect on and improve their practice, and take responsibility for identifying and meeting their developing professional needs. (b) Identify priorities for their early professional development in the context of induction.	
Q8	Have a creative and constructively critical approach towards innovation, being prepared to adapt their practice where benefits and improvements are identified.	
Q9	Act upon advice and feedback and be open to coaching and mentoring.	

For free downloads of all these forms go to www.ecmconnections.co.uk

2. Professional knowledge and understanding

Teaching and learning		Evidence
Q10	Have a knowledge and understanding of a range of teaching, learning and behaviour management strategies and know how to use and adapt them, including how to personalize learning and provide opportunities for all learners to achieve their potential.	
Assessment and monitoring		**Evidence**
Q11	Know the assessment requirements and arrangements for the subjects/curriculum areas they are trained to teach, including those relating to public examinations and qualifications.	
Q12	Know a range of approaches to assessment, including the importance of formative assessment.	
Q13	Know how to use local and national statistical information to evaluate the effectiveness of their teaching, to monitor the progress of those they teach and to raise levels of attainment.	
Subjects and curriculum		**Evidence**
Q14	Have a secure knowledge and understanding of their subjects/curriculum areas and related pedagogy to enable them to teach effectively across the age and ability range for which they are trained.	
Q15	Know and understand the relevant statutory and non-statutory curricula and frameworks, including those provided through the National Strategies, for their subjects/curriculum areas, and other relevant initiatives applicable to the age and ability range for which they are trained.	
Literacy, numeracy and ICT		**Evidence**
Q16	Have passed the professional skills tests in numeracy, literacy and information and communications technology (ICT).	
Q17	Know how to use skills in literacy, numeracy and ICT to support their teaching and wider professional activities.	

For free downloads of all these forms go to www.ecmconnections.co.uk

Achievement and diversity		Evidence
Q18	Understand how children and young people develop and how the progress, rate of development and well-being of learners are affected by a range of developmental, social, religious, ethnic, cultural and linguistic influences.	
Q19	Know how to make effective personalized provision for those they teach, including those for whom English is an additional language or who have special educational needs or disabilities, and how to take practical account of diversity and promote equality and inclusion in their teaching.	
Q20	Know and understand the roles of colleagues with specific responsibilities, including those with responsibility for learners with special educational needs and disabilities and other individual learning needs.	
Health and well-being		**Evidence**
Q21	(a) Be aware of the current legal requirements, national policies and guidance on the safeguarding and promotion of the well-being of children and young people. (b) Know how to identify and support children and young people whose progress, development or well-being is affected by changes or difficulties in their personal circumstances, and when to refer them to colleagues for specialist support.	

For free downloads of all these forms go to www.ecmconnections.co.uk

3. Professional skills

Planning		Evidence
Q22	Plan for progression across the age and ability range for which they are trained, designing effective learning sequences within lessons and across series of lessons and demonstrating secure subject/ curriculum knowledge.	
Q23	Design opportunities for learners to develop their literacy, numeracy and ICT skills.	
Q24	Plan homework or other out-of-class work to sustain learners' progress and to extend and consolidate their learning.	
Teaching		**Evidence**
Q25	Teach lessons and sequences of lessons across the age and ability range for which they are trained in which they: (a) use a range of teaching strategies and resources, including e-learning, taking practical account of diversity and promoting equality and inclusion (b) build on prior knowledge, develop concepts and processes, enable learners to apply new knowledge, understanding and skills and meet learning objectives (c) adapt their language to suit the learners they teach, introducing new ideas and concepts clearly, and using explanations, questions, discussions and plenaries effectively (d) demonstrate the ability to manage the learning of individuals, groups and whole classes, modifying their teaching to suit the stage of the lesson.	
Assessing, monitoring and giving feedback		**Evidence**
Q26	(a) Make effective use of a range of assessment, monitoring and recording strategies. (b) Assess the learning needs of those they teach in order to set challenging learning objectives.	
Q27	Provide timely, accurate and constructive feedback on learners' attainment, progress and areas for development.	
Q28	Support and guide learners to reflect on their learning, identify the progress they have made and identify their emerging learning needs.	

For free downloads of all these forms go to www.ecmconnections.co.uk

Reviewing teaching and learning		Evidence
Q29	Evaluate the impact of their teaching on the progress of all learners, and modify their planning and classroom practice where necessary.	
Learning environment		**Evidence**
Q30	Establish a purposeful and safe learning environment conducive to learning and identify opportunities for learners to learn in out-of-school contexts.	
Q31	Establish a clear framework for classroom discipline to manage learners' behaviour constructively and promote their self-control and independence.	
Team-working and collaboration		**Evidence**
Q32	Work as a team member and identify opportunities for working with colleagues, sharing the development of effective practice with them.	
Q33	Ensure that colleagues working with them are appropriately involved in supporting learning and understand the roles they are expected to fulfil.	

For free downloads of all these forms go to www.ecmconnections.co.uk

Effective Teachers in Primary Schools

Appendix 8: Professional Standards for Teachers – CORE Criteria

1. Professional attributes

Relationships with children and young people	
C1	Have high expectations of children and young people including a commitment to ensuring that they can achieve their full educational potential and to establishing fair, respectful, trusting, supportive and constructive relationships with them.
C2	Hold positive values and attitudes and adopt high standards of behaviour in their professional role.
Frameworks	
C3	Maintain an up-to-date knowledge and understanding of the professional duties of teachers and the statutory framework within which they work, and contribute to the development, implementation and evaluation of the policies and practice of their workplace, including those designed to promote equality of opportunity.
Communicating and working with others	
C4	(a) Communicate effectively with children, young people and colleagues. (b) Communicate effectively with parents and carers, conveying timely and relevant information about attainment, objectives, progress and well-being. (c) Recognize that communication is a two-way process and encourage parents and carers to participate in discussions about the progress, development and well-being of children and young people.
C5	Recognize and respect the contributions that colleagues, parents and carers can make to the development and well-being of children and young people, and to raising their levels of attainment.
C6	Have a commitment to collaboration and co-operative working, where appropriate.
Personal professional development	
C7	Evaluate their performance and be committed to improving their practice through appropriate professional development.
C8	Have a creative and constructively critical approach towards innovation; being prepared to adapt their practice where benefits and improvements are identified.
C9	Act upon advice and feedback and be open to coaching and mentoring.

For free downloads of all these forms go to www.ecmconnections.co.uk

---

2. Professional knowledge and understanding

Teaching and learning	
C10	Have a good, up-to-date working knowledge and understanding of a range of teaching, learning and behaviour management strategies and know how to use and adapt them, including how to personalize learning to provide opportunities for all learners to achieve their potential.
Assessment and monitoring	
C11	Know the assessment requirements and arrangements for the subjects/curriculum areas they teach, including those relating to public examinations and qualifications.
C12	Know a range of approaches to assessment, including the importance of formative assessment.
C13	Know how to use local and national statistical information to evaluate the effectiveness of their teaching, to monitor the progress of those they teach and to raise levels of attainment.
C14	Know how to use reports and other sources of external information related to assessment in order to provide learners with accurate and constructive feedback on their strengths, weaknesses, attainment, progress and areas for development, including action plans for improvement.
Subjects and curriculum	
C15	Have a secure knowledge and understanding of their subjects/curriculum areas and related pedagogy including: the contribution that their subjects/curriculum areas can make to cross-curricular learning; and recent relevant developments.
C16	Know and understand the relevant statutory and non-statutory curricula and frameworks, including those provided through the National Strategies, for their subjects/curriculum areas and other relevant initiatives across the age and ability range they teach.
Literacy, numeracy and ICT	
C17	Know how to use skills in literacy, numeracy and ICT to support their teaching and wider professional activities.
Achievement and diversity	
C18	Understand how children and young people develop and how the progress, rate of development and well-being of learners are affected by a range of developmental, social, religious, ethnic, cultural and linguistic influences.
C19	Know how to make effective personalized provision for those they teach, including those for whom English is an additional language or who have special educational needs or disabilities, and how to take practical account of diversity and promote equality and inclusion in their teaching.
C20	Understand the roles of colleagues such as those having specific responsibilities for learners with special educational needs, disabilities and other individual learning needs, and the contributions they can make to the learning, development and well-being of children and young people.
C21	Know when to draw on the expertise of colleagues, such as those with responsibility for the safeguarding of children and young people with special educational needs and disabilities, and to refer to sources of information, advice and support from external agencies.

For free downloads of all these forms go to www.ecmconnections.co.uk

Health and well-being	
C22	Know the current legal requirements, national policies and guidance on the safeguarding and promotion of the well-being of children and young people.
C23	Know the local arrangements concerning the safeguarding of children and young people.
C24	Know how to identify potential child abuse or neglect and follow safeguarding procedures.
C25	Know how to identify and support children and young people whose progress, development or well-being is affected by changes or difficulties in their personal circumstances, and when to refer them to colleagues for specialist support.

For free downloads of all these forms go to www.ecmconnections.co.uk

3. Professional skills

Planning	
C26	Plan for progression across the age and ability range they teach, designing effective learning sequences within lessons and across series of lessons informed by secure subject/curriculum knowledge.
C27	Design opportunities for learners to develop their literacy, numeracy, ICT and thinking and learning skills appropriate within their phase and context.
C28	Plan, set and assess homework, other out-of-class assignments and coursework for examinations, where appropriate, to sustain learners' progress and to extend and consolidate their learning.
Teaching	
C29	Teach challenging, well-organized lessons and sequences of lessons across the age and ability range they teach in which they: (a) use an appropriate range of teaching strategies and resources, including e-learning, which meet learners' needs and take practical account of diversity and promote equality and inclusion (b) build on the prior knowledge and attainment of those they teach in order that learners meet learning objectives and make sustained progress (c) develop concepts and processes which enable learners to apply new knowledge, understanding and skills (d) adapt their language to suit the learners they teach, introducing new ideas and concepts clearly, and using explanations, questions, discussions and plenaries effectively (e) manage the learning of individuals, groups and whole classes effectively, modifying their teaching appropriately to suit the stage of the lesson and the needs of the learners.
C30	Teach engaging and motivating lessons informed by well-grounded expectations of learners and designed to raise levels of attainment.
Assessing, monitoring and giving feedback	
C31	Make effective use of an appropriate range of observation, assessment, monitoring and recording strategies as a basis for setting challenging learning objectives and monitoring learners' progress and levels of attainment.
C32	Provide learners, colleagues, parents and carers with timely, accurate and constructive feedback on learners' attainment, progress and areas for development.
C33	Support and guide learners so that they can reflect on their learning, identify the progress they have made, set positive targets for improvement and become successful independent learners.
C34	Use assessment as part of their teaching to diagnose learners' needs, set realistic and challenging targets for improvement and plan future teaching.
Reviewing teaching and learning	
C35	Review the effectiveness of their teaching and its impact on learners' progress, attainment and well-being, refining their approaches where necessary.
C36	Review the impact of the feedback provided to learners and guide learners on how to improve their attainment.

For free downloads of all these forms go to www.ecmconnections.co.uk

	Learning environment
C37	(a) Establish a purposeful and safe learning environment which complies with current legal requirements, national policies and guidance on the safeguarding and well-being of children and young people so that learners feel secure and sufficiently confident to make an active contribution to learning and to the school. (b) Make use of the local arrangements concerning the safeguarding of children and young people. (c) Identify and use opportunities to personalize and extend learning through out-of-school contexts where possible making links between in-school learning and learning in out-of-school contexts.
C38	(a) Manage learners' behaviour constructively by establishing and maintaining a clear and positive framework for discipline, in line with the school's behaviour policy. (b) Use a range of behaviour management techniques and strategies, adapting them as necessary to promote the self-control and independence of learners.
C39	Promote learners' self-control, independence and cooperation through developing their social, emotional and behavioural skills.
	Team working and collaboration
C40	Work as a team member and identify opportunities for working with colleagues, managing their work where appropriate and sharing the development of effective practice with them.
C41	Ensure that colleagues working with them are appropriately involved in supporting learning and understand the roles they are expected to fulfil.

For free downloads of all these forms go to www.ecmconnections.co.uk

Appendix 9: Professional Standards for Teachers – CORE Forms

1. Professional attributes

Relationships with children and young people		Evidence
C1	Have high expectations of children and young people including a commitment to ensuring that they can achieve their full educational potential and to establishing fair, respectful, trusting, supportive and constructive relationships with them.	
C2	Hold positive values and attitudes and adopt high standards of behaviour in their professional role	
Frameworks		**Evidence**
C3	Maintain an up-to-date knowledge and understanding of the professional duties of teachers and the statutory framework within which they work, and contribute to the development, implementation and evaluation of the policies and practice of their workplace, including those designed to promote equality of opportunity.	
Communicating and working with others		**Evidence**
C4	(a) Communicate effectively with children, young people and colleagues. (b) Communicate effectively with parents and carers, conveying timely and relevant information about attainment, objectives, progress and well-being. (c) Recognize that communication is a two-way process and encourage parents and carers to participate in discussions about the progress, development and well-being of children and young people.	
C5	Recognize and respect the contributions that colleagues, parents and carers can make to the development and well-being of children and young people, and to raising their levels of attainment.	
C6	Have a commitment to collaboration and co-operative working, where appropriate.	
Personal professional development		**Evidence**
C7	Evaluate their performance and be committed to improving their practice through appropriate professional development.	
C8	Have a creative and constructively critical approach towards innovation; being prepared to adapt their practice where benefits and improvements are identified.	
C9	Act upon advice and feedback and be open to coaching and mentoring.	

For free downloads of all these forms go to www.ecmconnections.co.uk

2. Professional knowledge and understanding

Teaching and learning		Evidence
C10	Have a good, up-to-date working knowledge and understanding of a range of teaching, learning and behaviour management strategies and know how to use and adapt them, including how to personalize learning to provide opportunities for all learners to achieve their potential.	
Assessment and monitoring		**Evidence**
C11	Know the assessment requirements and arrangements for the subjects/curriculum areas they teach, including those relating to public examinations and qualifications.	
C12	Know a range of approaches to assessment, including the importance of formative assessment.	
C13	Know how to use local and national statistical information to evaluate the effectiveness of their teaching, to monitor the progress of those they teach and to raise levels of attainment.	
C14	Know how to use reports and other sources of external information related to assessment in order to provide learners with accurate and constructive feedback on their strengths, weaknesses, attainment, progress and areas for development, including action plans for improvement.	
Subjects and curriculum		**Evidence**
C15	Have a secure knowledge and understanding of their subjects/curriculum areas and related pedagogy including: the contribution that their subjects/curriculum areas can make to cross-curricular learning; and recent relevant developments.	
C16	Know and understand the relevant statutory and non-statutory curricula and frameworks, including those provided through the National Strategies, for their subjects/curriculum areas and other relevant initiatives across the age and ability range they teach.	
Literacy, numeracy and ICT		**Evidence**
C17	Know how to use skills in literacy, numeracy and ICT to support their teaching and wider professional activities.	
Achievement and diversity		**Evidence**
C18	Understand how children and young people develop and how the progress, rate of development and well-being of learners are affected by a range of developmental, social, religious, ethnic, cultural and linguistic influences.	

For free downloads of all these forms go to www.ecmconnections.co.uk

---

C19	Know how to make effective personalized provision for those they teach, including those for whom English is an additional language or who have special educational needs or disabilities, and how to take practical account of diversity and promote equality and inclusion in their teaching.	
C20	Understand the roles of colleagues such as those having specific responsibilities for learners with special educational needs, disabilities and other individual learning needs, and the contributions they can make to the learning, development and well-being of children and young people.	
C21	Know when to draw on the expertise of colleagues, such as those with responsibility for the safeguarding of children and young people with special educational needs and disabilities, and to refer to sources of information, advice and support from external agencies.	
Health and well-being		**Evidence**
C22	Know the current legal requirements, national policies and guidance on the safeguarding and promotion of the well-being of children and young people.	
C23	Know the local arrangements concerning the safeguarding of children and young people.	
C24	Know how to identify potential child abuse or neglect and follow safeguarding procedures.	
C25	Know how to identify and support children and young people whose progress, development or well-being is affected by changes or difficulties in their personal circumstances, and when to refer them to colleagues for specialist support.	

For free downloads of all these forms go to www.ecmconnections.co.uk

Effective Teachers in Primary Schools

3. Professional skills

Planning		Evidence
C26	Plan for progression across the age and ability range they teach, designing effective learning sequences within lessons and across series of lessons informed by secure subject/ curriculum knowledge.	
C27	Design opportunities for learners to develop their literacy, numeracy, ICT and thinking and learning skills appropriate within their phase and context.	
C28	Plan, set and assess homework, other out-of-class assignments and coursework for examinations, where appropriate, to sustain learners' progress and to extend and consolidate their learning.	
Teaching		**Evidence**
C29	Teach challenging, well-organized lessons and sequences of lessons across the age and ability range they teach in which they: (a) use an appropriate range of teaching strategies and resources, including e-learning, which meet learners' needs and take practical account of diversity and promote equality and inclusion (b) build on the prior knowledge and attainment of those they teach in order that learners meet learning objectives and make sustained progress (c) develop concepts and processes which enable learners to apply new knowledge, understanding and skills (d) adapt their language to suit the learners they teach, introducing new ideas and concepts clearly, and using explanations, questions, discussions and plenaries effectively (e) manage the learning of individuals, groups and whole classes effectively, modifying their teaching appropriately to suit the stage of the lesson and the needs of the learners.	
C30	Teach engaging and motivating lessons informed by well-grounded expectations of learners and designed to raise levels of attainment.	
Assessing, monitoring and giving feedback		**Evidence**
C31	Make effective use of an appropriate range of observation, assessment, monitoring and recording strategies as a basis for setting challenging learning objectives and monitoring learners' progress and levels of attainment.	

For free downloads of all these forms go to www.ecmconnections.co.uk

C32	Provide learners, colleagues, parents and carers with timely, accurate and constructive feedback on learners' attainment, progress and areas for development.	
C33	Support and guide learners so that they can reflect on their learning, identify the progress they have made, set positive targets for improvement and become successful independent learners.	
C34	Use assessment as part of their teaching to diagnose learners' needs, set realistic and challenging targets for improvement and plan future teaching.	
Reviewing teaching and learning		**Evidence**
C35	Review the effectiveness of their teaching and its impact on learners' progress, attainment and well-being, refining their approaches where necessary.	
C36	Review the impact of the feedback provided to learners and guide learners on how to improve their attainment.	
Learning environment		**Evidence**
C37	(a) Establish a purposeful and safe learning environment which complies with current legal requirements, national policies and guidance on the safeguarding and well-being of children and young people so that learners feel secure and sufficiently confident to make an active contribution to learning and to the school. (b) Make use of the local arrangements concerning the safeguarding of children and young people. (c) Identify and use opportunities to personalize and extend learning through out-of-school contexts where possible making links between in-school learning and learning in out-of-school contexts.	
C38	(a) Manage learners' behaviour constructively by establishing and maintaining a clear and positive framework for discipline, in line with the school's behaviour policy. (b) Use a range of behaviour management techniques and strategies, adapting them as necessary to promote the self-control and independence of learners.	
C39	Promote learners' self-control, independence and cooperation through developing their social, emotional and behavioural skills.	

For free downloads of all these forms go to www.ecmconnections.co.uk

Teamworking and collaboration		Evidence
C40	Work as a team member and identify opportunities for working with colleagues, managing their work where appropriate and sharing the development of effective practice with them.	
C41	Ensure that colleagues working with them are appropriately involved in supporting learning and understand the roles they are expected to fulfil.	

For free downloads of all these forms go to www.ecmconnections.co.uk

Appendix 10: Professional Standards for Teachers – Post Threshold Criteria

1. Professional attributes

Relationships with children and young people	
Frameworks	
P1	Contribute significantly, where appropriate, to implementing workplace policies and practice and to promoting collective responsibility for their implementation.
Communicating and working with others	
Personal professional development	

For free downloads of all these forms go to www.ecmconnections.co.uk

2. Professional knowledge and understanding

Teaching and learning	
P2	Have an extensive knowledge and understanding of how to use and adapt a range of teaching, learning and behaviour management strategies, including how to personalize learning to provide opportunities for all learners to achieve their potential.
Assessment and monitoring	
P3	Have an extensive knowledge and well-informed understanding of the assessment requirements and arrangements for the subjects/curriculum areas they teach, including those related to public examinations and qualifications.
P4	Have up-to-date knowledge and understanding of the different types of qualification and specification and their suitability for meeting learners' needs.
Subjects and curriculum	
P5	Have a more developed knowledge and understanding of their subjects/curriculum areas and related pedagogy including how learning progresses within them.
Literacy, numeracy and ICT	
Achievement and diversity	
Health and well-being	
P6	Have sufficient depth of knowledge and experience to be able to give advice on the development and well-being of children and young people.

For free downloads of all these forms go to www.ecmconnections.co.uk

3. Professional skills

Planning	
P7	Be flexible, creative and adept at designing learning sequences within lessons and across lessons that are effective and consistently well-matched to learning objectives and the needs of learners, and which integrate recent developments, including those relating to subject/curriculum knowledge.
Teaching	
P8	Have teaching skills that lead to learners achieving well relative to their prior attainment, making progress as good as, or better than, similar learners nationally.
Assessing, monitoring and giving feedback	
Reviewing teaching and learning	
Learning environment	
Teamworking and collaboration	
P9	Promote collaboration and work effectively as a team member.
P10	Contribute to the professional development of colleagues through coaching and mentoring, demonstrating effective practice, and providing advice and feedback.

For free downloads of all these forms go to www.ecmconnections.co.uk

Appendix 11: Professional Standards for Teachers – Post Threshold Forms

1. Professional attributes

Relationships with children and young people	
Frameworks	**Evidence**
P1	Contribute significantly, where appropriate, to implementing workplace policies and practice and to promoting collective responsibility for their implementation.	
Communicating and working with others	
Personal professional development	

For free downloads of all these forms go to www.ecmconnections.co.uk

2. Professional knowledge and understanding

Teaching and learning		Evidence
P2	Have an extensive knowledge and understanding of how to use and adapt a range of teaching, learning and behaviour management strategies, including how to personalize learning to provide opportunities for all learners to achieve their potential.	
Assessment and monitoring		**Evidence**
P3	Have an extensive knowledge and well-informed understanding of the assessment requirements and arrangements for the subjects/curriculum areas they teach, including those related to public examinations and qualifications.	
P4	Have up-to-date knowledge and understanding of the different types of qualification and specification and their suitability for meeting learners' needs.	
Subjects and curriculum		**Evidence**
P5	Have a more developed knowledge and understanding of their subjects/curriculum areas and related pedagogy including how learning progresses within them.	
Literacy, numeracy and ICT		
Achievement and diversity		
Health and well-being		**Evidence**
P6	Have sufficient depth of knowledge and experience to be able to give advice on the development and well-being of children and young people.	

For free downloads of all these forms go to www.ecmconnections.co.uk

3. Professional skills

Planning		Evidence
P7	Be flexible, creative and adept at designing learning sequences within lessons and across lessons that are effective and consistently well-matched to learning objectives and the needs of learners, and which integrate recent developments, including those relating to subject/curriculum knowledge.	
Teaching		**Evidence**
P8	Have teaching skills that lead to learners achieving well relative to their prior attainment, making progress as good as, or better than, similar learners nationally.	
Assessing, monitoring and giving feedback		
Reviewing teaching and learning		
Learning environment		
Team working and collaboration		**Evidence**
P9	Promote collaboration and work effectively as a team member.	
P10	Contribute to the professional development of colleagues through coaching and mentoring, demonstrating effective practice, and providing advice and feedback.	

For free downloads of all these forms go to www.ecmconnections.co.uk

Appendix 12: Professional Standards for Teachers – Excellent Teacher Criteria

1. Professional attributes

Relationships with children and young people	
Frameworks	
E1	Be willing to take a leading role in developing workplace policies and practice and in promoting collective responsibility for their implementation.
Communicating and working with others	
Personal professional development	
E2	Research and evaluate innovative curricular practices and draw on research outcomes and other sources of external evidence to inform their own practice and that of colleagues.

For free downloads of all these forms go to www.ecmconnections.co.uk

2. Professional knowledge and understanding

Teaching and learning	
E3	Have a critical understanding of the most effective teaching, learning and behaviour management strategies, including how to select and use approaches that personalize learning to provide opportunities for all learners to achieve their potential.
Assessment and monitoring	
E4	Know how to improve the effectiveness of assessment practice in the workplace, including how to analyse statistical information to evaluate the effectiveness of teaching and learning across the school.
Subjects and curriculum	
E5	Have an extensive and deep knowledge and understanding of their subjects/curriculum areas and related pedagogy gained, for example, through involvement in wider professional networks associated with their subjects/curriculum areas.
Literacy, numeracy and ICT	
Achievement and diversity	
E6	Have an extensive knowledge on matters concerning equality, inclusion and diversity in teaching.
Health and well-being	

For free downloads of all these forms go to www.ecmconnections.co.uk

3. Professional skills

Planning	
E7	(a) Take a lead in planning collaboratively with colleagues in order to promote effective practice. (b) Identify and explore links within and between subjects/curriculum areas in their planning.
Teaching	
E8	Have teaching skills that lead to excellent results and outcomes.
E9	Demonstrate excellent and innovative pedagogical practice.
Assessing, monitoring and giving feedback	
E10	Demonstrate excellent ability to assess and evaluate.
E11	Have an excellent ability to provide learners, colleagues, parents and carers with timely, accurate and constructive feedback on learners' attainment, progress and areas for development that promotes pupil progress.
Reviewing teaching and learning	
E12	Use local and national statistical data and other information, in order to provide: (a) a comparative baseline for evaluating learners' progress and attainment (b) a means of judging the effectiveness of their teaching, and (c) a basis for improving teaching and learning.
Learning environment	
Teamworking and collaboration	
E13	Work closely with leadership teams, taking a leading role in developing, implementing and evaluating policies and practice that contribute to school improvement.
E14	Contribute to the professional development of colleagues using a broad range of techniques and skills appropriate to their needs so that they demonstrate enhanced and effective practice.
E15	Make well-founded appraisals of situations upon which they are asked to advise, applying high level skills in classroom observation to evaluate and advise colleagues on their work and devising and implementing effective strategies to meet the learning needs of children and young people leading to improvements in pupil outcomes.

For free downloads of all these forms go to www.ecmconnections.co.uk

Appendix 13: Professional Standards for Teachers – Excellent Teacher Forms

1. Professional attributes

Relationships with children and young people	
Frameworks	**Evidence**
E1 Be willing to take a leading role in developing workplace policies and practice and in promoting collective responsibility for their implementation.	
Communicating and working with others	
Personal professional development	**Evidence**
E2 Research and evaluate innovative curricular practices and draw on research outcomes and other sources of external evidence to inform their own practice and that of colleagues.	

For free downloads of all these forms go to www.ecmconnections.co.uk

2. Professional knowledge and understanding

Teaching and learning		Evidence
E3	Have a critical understanding of the most effective teaching, learning and behaviour management strategies, including how to select and use approaches that personalize learning to provide opportunities for all learners to achieve their potential.	
Assessment and monitoring		**Evidence**
E4	Know how to improve the effectiveness of assessment practice in the workplace, including how to analyse statistical information to evaluate the effectiveness of teaching and learning across the school.	
Subjects and curriculum		**Evidence**
E5	Have an extensive and deep knowledge and understanding of their subjects/curriculum areas and related pedagogy gained, for example, through involvement in wider professional networks associated with their subjects/curriculum areas.	
Literacy, numeracy and ICT		
Achievement and diversity		**Evidence**
E6	Have an extensive knowledge on matters concerning equality, inclusion and diversity in teaching.	
Health and well-being		

For free downloads of all these forms go to www.ecmconnections.co.uk

3. Professional skills

Planning		Evidence
E7	(a) Take a lead in planning collaboratively with colleagues in order to promote effective practice. (b) Identify and explore links within and between subjects/curriculum areas in their planning.	
Teaching		**Evidence**
E8	Have teaching skills that lead to excellent results and outcomes.	
E9	Demonstrate excellent and innovative pedagogical practice.	
Assessing, monitoring and giving feedback		**Evidence**
E10	Demonstrate excellent ability to assess and evaluate.	
E11	Have an excellent ability to provide learners, colleagues, parents and carers with timely, accurate and constructive feedback on learners' attainment, progress and areas for development that promotes pupil progress.	
Reviewing teaching and learning		**Evidence**
E12	Use local and national statistical data and other information, in order to provide: (a) a comparative baseline for evaluating learners' progress and attainment (b) a means of judging the effectiveness of their teaching, and (c) a basis for improving teaching and learning.	
Learning environment		
Teamworking and collaboration		**Evidence**
E13	Work closely with leadership teams, taking a leading role in developing, implementing and evaluating policies and practice that contribute to school improvement.	
E14	Contribute to the professional development of colleagues using a broad range of techniques and skills appropriate to their needs so that they demonstrate enhanced and effective practice.	

For free downloads of all these forms go to www.ecmconnections.co.uk

E15	Make well-founded appraisals of situations upon which they are asked to advise, applying high level skills in classroom observation to evaluate and advise colleagues on their work and devising and implementing effective strategies to meet the learning needs of children and young people leading to improvements in pupil outcomes.	

For free downloads of all these forms go to www.ecmconnections.co.uk

Appendix 14: Professional Standards for Teachers – Advanced Skills Teacher Criteria

1. Professional attributes

Relationships with children and young people	
Frameworks	
A1	Be willing to take on a strategic leadership role in developing workplace policies and practice and in promoting collective responsibility for their implementation in their own and other workplaces.
Communicating and working with others	
Personal professional development	

For free downloads of all these forms go to www.ecmconnections.co.uk

2. Professional knowledge and understanding

Teaching and learning	
Assessment and monitoring	
Subjects and curriculum	
Literacy, numeracy and ICT	
Achievement and diversity	
Health and well-being	

For free downloads of all these forms go to www.ecmconnections.co.uk

Effective Teachers in Primary Schools

3. Professional skills

Planning	
Teaching	
Assessing, monitoring and giving feedback	
Reviewing teaching and learning	
Learning environment	
Teamworking and collaboration	
A2	Be part of or work closely with leadership teams, taking a leadership role in developing, implementing and evaluating policies and practice in their own and other workplaces that contribute to school improvement.
A3	Possess the analytical, interpersonal and organizational skills necessary to work effectively with staff and leadership teams beyond their own school.

For free downloads of all these forms go to www.ecmconnections.co.uk

Appendix 15: Professional Standards for Teachers – Advanced Skills Teacher Forms

1. Professional attributes

Relationships with children and young people	
Frameworks	**Evidence**
A1 Be willing to take on a strategic leadership role in developing workplace policies and practice and in promoting collective responsibility for their implementation in their own and other workplaces.	
Communicating and working with others	
Personal professional development	

For free downloads of all these forms go to www.ecmconnections.co.uk

2. Professional knowledge and understanding

Teaching and learning	
Assessment and monitoring	
Subjects and curriculum	
Literacy, numeracy and ICT	
Achievement and diversity	
Health and well-being	

For free downloads of all these forms go to www.ecmconnections.co.uk

3. Professional skills

Planning	
Teaching	
Assessing, monitoring and giving feedback	
Reviewing teaching and learning	
Learning environment	

Teamworking and collaboration		Evidence
A2	Be part of or work closely with leadership teams, taking a leadership role in developing, implementing and evaluating policies and practice in their own and other workplaces that contribute to school improvement.	
A3	Possess the analytical, interpersonal and organizational skills necessary to work effectively with staff and leadership teams beyond their own school.	

For free downloads of all these forms go to www.ecmconnections.co.uk

Appendix 16: Threshold Application Forms

EXAMPLE 1: BLANK THRESHOLD ASSESSMENT APPLICATION FORM

> **IMPORTANT: PLEASE READ THE ENCLOSED GUIDANCE NOTES BEFORE STARTING TO COMPLETE THE APPLICATION FORM. This form is also available electronically on the Internet at www.dfee.gov.uk/teachingreforms**

> **THIS APPLICATION FORM SHOULD BE HANDLED IN CONFIDENCE AT ALL TIMES.**
>
> **Access to this form will be restricted to those who are playing a part in the assessment and verification process.**

Personal Details

Surname   First Name(s)

Home Address/Telephone/e:mail/fax

DfEE/Welsh Office Teacher Reference Number

Career Details

Current post

Date joined present school   Length in Post

If not in school, current post and last teaching post (please give dates)

Subject or area specialism, if relevant

Name and Location of School (or other employer)

Name of head

Primary   Secondary   Other

Equal Opportunities Monitoring

The DfEE is committed to equal opportunities. We would like to monitor the profile of those applying for threshold assessment and the outcomes.

To enable us to do this, please complete the enclosed equal opportunities questionnaire and pass it to your headteacher who will forward it with your application form. The information you give us will be treated as confidential and will not form part of the application process.

Data Protection Act 1998

The Department for Education and Employment will process the information collected in this document for the purpose of assessing and monitoring teachers' applications to cross the performance threshold. This information will be processed only within the terms of the Department's Data Protection notification.

1. KNOWLEDGE AND UNDERSTANDING

Please summarise evidence that you:

- have a thorough and up-to-date knowledge of the teaching of your subject(s) and take account of wider curriculum developments which are relevant to your work.

Assessment by headteacher, noting any areas for further development.

Standard Met/Not Yet Met

2. TEACHING AND ASSESSMENT

Please summarise evidence

- plan lessons and sequences of lessons to meet pupils' individual learning needs

- use a range of appropriate strategies for teaching and classroom management

- use information about prior attainment to set well-grounded expectations for pupils and monitor progress to give clear and constructive feedback.

(continue on a second page if necessary)

Assessment by headteacher, noting any areas for further development. Each of the three standards above must be met.

3. PUPIL PROGRESS

Please summarise evidence that
relative to their prior attainment, making progress as good as or better than similar pupils nationally. This should be shown in marks or grades in any relevant national tests or examinations, or school based assessment for pupils where national tests and examinations are not taken.

Assessment by headteacher, noting any areas for further development.

Standard Met/Net Yet Met

Effective Teachers in Primary Schools

4. WIDER PROFESSIONAL EFFECTIVENESS

Please summarise evidence that you:

- **take responsibility for your professional development and use the outcomes to improve your teaching and pupils' learning**

- **make an active contribution to the policies and aspirations of your school.**

Assessment by headteacher, noting any areas for further development. Both standards must be met.

Standards Met/Not Yet Met

5. PROFESSIONAL CHARACTERISTICS

Much of what you have said earlier in this form will give information about the professional characteristics you show in your teaching. Please give any further examples here of how you:

challenge and support all pupils to do their best through

> **inspiring trust and confidence**
> **building team commitment**
> **engaging and motivating pupils**
> **analytical thinking**
> **positive action to improve the quality of pupils' learning.**

Assessment by headteacher, taking account of each aspect above and noting any areas for further development.

Standard Met/Net Yet Met

Declaration by applicant

I certify that I am eligible for assessment and that the information in this form is correct. I would like the evidence I have presented to be taken into account in assessing my work against the threshold standards. I understand that further pay progression on the upper pay range will be awarded on the basis of performance and accept that my annual reviews will be used to inform such judgements.

Signed .... Date ....

Declaration by headteacher (or equivalent if not in school)

Applicant name: ……………………………..

School: …………………………………………

Please explain what evidence additional to this form you have taken into account, e.g. discussion with team leader, appraisal/performance review. Note how the evidence takes account of classroom performance. Set the teacher's performance in the overall context of the achievements of your school. Indicate whether, to the best of your knowledge, the information provided by the applicant is correct, that it derives from the applicant's own practice, and is representative of their overall performance.

Please make a final recommendation in the relevant box below. To be successful applicants

Threshold Standards Met ❏

Not yet Met-2 pt ❏

Signed ……………………………………………… Date ………………………………………

Print name ……………………………………….. School name …………………………………

Appendix 17: OFSTED-style Forms

1. Evidence form

Inspector's OIN		School URN		Observation type	L A D O
Year group(s)		Grouping	A M G S B O	Present/NOR	
Subject codes		Accreditation	GC AL AS VA VI VF VP VO XO	Observation time	
Teacher's status	QUTSN	Lesson type	CL GR IN MI XO	Support teacher/staff	
Teacher's code		Insp's EF No.		SIS Input Ref. No.	

Context

Evidence

When recording grades, use 0 to 7 to reflect judgements in the text on: Teaching; Learning; Attainment; Attitudes and behaviour:

Teaching		Learning		Attainment		Attitudes and behaviour	

2. Lesson observation aid

Context

Briefly describe the lesson and what pupils are doing.

Evidence

Record the evidence you have collected and your judgements made on the basis of that evidence.

Use evaluative words carefully to distinguish, for example, between very good and good, so that someone else would arrive at the same grade and evaluation:

1 = **excellent**

2 = **very good**

3 = **good**

4 = **satisfactory**

5 = **unsatisfactory**

6 = **poor**

7 = **very poor**

0 = **no evidence.**

Synonyms allow for varied, more interesting writing – for example:

▸ excellent = outstanding, superb

▸ satisfactory = competent, acceptable

and so forth.

Focus on strengths and weaknesses of the lesson and indicate what makes them strengths or weaknesses.

Give illustrations that you can draw on for examples of strengths and weaknesses when giving feedback on the lesson.

Give clear judgements, in accordance with the criteria in the OFSTED Handbook, especially on Teaching, Learning, Attainments and Attitudes and behaviour. Write in notes or in continuous prose.

Use all relevant criteria for which you have evidence.

Bibliography

Blasé, J. and Blasé, J. (1998) *Handbook of Instructional Leadership: How Really Good Principles Promote Teaching and Learning* (Thousand Oaks, California: Corwin Press), extract reprinted by permission of Corwin Press Inc

Broadfoot, P. (2000) 'The BERA Stenhouse Lecture, 1999', in *Culture Learning and Comparison* (Nottingham: British Educational Research Association)

Buckingham, M. and Coffman, C. (2001) *First, Break all the Rules* (London: Simon and Schuster)

Busher, H., Harris, A. *et al.* (2000) *Subject Leadership and School Improvement* (London: Paul Chapman Publishing), extract reprinted by permission of Sage Publications Ltd

Cordingley, P. (2002) *Recent practitioner-based developments in research and pedagogy* (Cambridge: Teaching and Learning Research Programme)

Covey, S. (1999) *The Seven Habits of Highly Effective People* (London: Simon and Schuster)

Davis, B. and Sumara, D. J. (1997) 'Cognition, Complexity and Teacher Education', *Harvard Educational Review*, spring 1997, 67 (1) 105–126, ©1997 by the President and Fellows of Harvard College. All rights reserved

Delors, J. *et al.* (1996) *Learning: The Treasure Within – Report to UNESCO of the International Commission on Education for the Twenty-First Century* (Paris: UNESCO), extract reprinted by permission of UNESCO

DfEE (2000) *A Model of Teacher Effectiveness: Report by Hay McBer to the Department for Education and Employment, June 2000* (London: HMSO), see www.teachernet.gov.uk/haymcber

DfES (2002) *Time for Standards: Reforming the school workforce* (DfES/0751/2002, November 2002), see www.teachernet.gov.uk/Management/staffinganddevelopment/remodelling

Dryden, G. and Vos, J. (2001) *The Learning Revolution* (Stafford: Network Educational Press)

Flecknoe, M. (2002) *School Effectiveness: Is this what we should seek?* (Contact m.flecknoe@lmu.ac.uk)

Flecknoe, M. (2002) *The changes that count in securing school improvement* (Contact m.flecknoe@lmu.ac.uk)

Flecknoe, M. (2002) *How ICT can help us to improve education.* Paper presented at AERA 2002, New Orleans (Contact m.flecknoe@lmu.ac.uk)

Flecknoe, M. (2002) *Where does the light come from? Reflective writing under the microscope* (Contact m.flecknoe@lmu.ac.uk)

Fraser, B. J. (1989) 'Research Syntheses on School and Instructional Effectiveness', in Creemers, B. P. M. and Scheerens, J. (eds), *International Journal of Educational Research*, 13

Fullan, M. (2001) *Leading in a Culture of Change* (Hoboken, New Jersey: Jossey-Bass), extract reprinted by permission of John Wiley & Sons, Inc

Gardner, H. (1993) *Frames of Mind* (New York: Basic Books) Gardner, H. (2002) 'Pick a brain', from Karen Gold's interview with Howard Gardner in *TES Friday Magazine*, 20 September 2002

Goleman, D. (1996) *Emotional Intelligence* (London: Bloomsbury Publishing), extract reprinted by permission of Bloomsbury Publishing

Goleman, D. (1999), interviewed in the *Times Educational Supplement* (4 June 1999)

Hargreaves, A. (1998) 'The Emotional Politics of Teaching and Teacher Development: with implications for educational leadership', *International Journal of Leadership in Education*, 1 (4) 315–316

Honey, P. and Munford, A. (1986) *The Manual of Learning Styles*, 2nd edition (Maidenhead: Peter Honey Publications)

Lortie, D. C. (1975) *Schoolteacher* (Chicago: University of Chicago Press)

Miliband, D. (2002) 'Can do better', *Teaching Today*, (the NASUWT's magazine for members), 33

Norretranders, T. (1998) *The User Illusion: Cutting consciousness down to size* (New York: Penguin)

Pickering, J. (1997) 'Involving pupils', *Research Matters* (Institute of Education, University of London: School Improvement Network), 6

Rosenholtz, S. J. (1989) 'Workplace Conditions That Affect Teacher Quality and Commitment: implications for teacher induction programs', *The Elementary School Journal*, 89 (4) 420–439

Ruddock, J., Chaplin, R. *et al.* (1996) *School Improvement: What can pupils tell us?* (London: David Fulton Publishers)

Rudow, B. (1999) 'Stress and Burnout in the Teaching Profession: European studies, issues, and research perspectives', in Vandenberghe, R. and Huberman, A. M. (eds), *Understanding and Preventing Teacher Burnout: A Sourcebook of International Research and Practice* (Cambridge: Cambridge University Press)

Sammons, P., Hillman, J. and Mortimore, P. (1995) *Key Characteristics of Effective Schools: a review of school effectiveness research* (London: OFSTED)

Scheerens, J. (1992) *Effective Schooling: research, theory and practice* (London: Cassell)

Skinner, B. F., in *New Scientist*, 21 May 1964

Smith, A. (1996) *Accelerated Learning in the Classroom* (Stafford: Network Educational Press)

Sternberg, R. J. (1985) *Beyond IQ: A triarchic theory of human intelligence* (New York: Cambridge University Press)

Townsend, T., Clarke, P. *et al.* (1999) *Perspectives on School Effectiveness and Improvement* (London: Institute of Education, University of London)

Watkins, C. (2000) *Managing Classroom Behaviour – from research to diagnosis* (London: Institute of Education, University of London, with the Association of Teachers and Lecturers)

Watkins, C. and Mortimore, C. (1999) 'Pedagogy: what do we know?', in Mortimore, P., *Understanding Pedagogy and its impact on learning* (London: Paul Chapman), extract reprinted by permission of Sage Publications Ltd

White, J. and Barber, M. (1997) *Perspectives on School Effectiveness and Improvement* (London: Institute of Education, University of London)